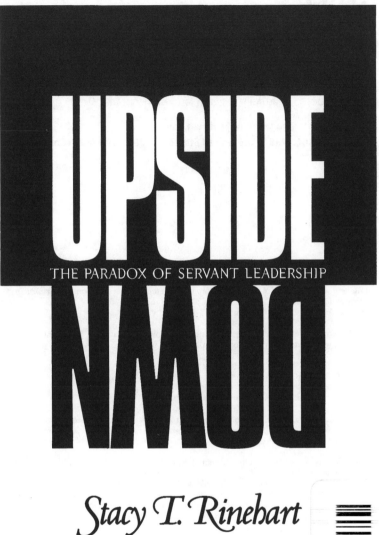

UPSIDE

THE PARADOX OF SERVANT LEADERSHIP

DOWN

Stacy T. Rinehart

NAVPRESS

NAVPRESS⬤.

NavPress is the publishing ministry of The Navigators, an international Christian organization and leader in personal spiritual development. NavPress is committed to helping people grow spiritually and enjoy lives of meaning and hope through personal and group resources that are biblically rooted, culturally relevant, and highly practical.

For a free catalog go to www.NavPress.com
or call 1.800.366.7788 in the United States or 1.800.839.4769 in Canada.

ISBN-13: 978-1-57683-079-6

Cover design: by Dan Jamison

Some of the anecdotal illustrations in this book are true to life and are included with the permission of the persons involved. All other illustrations are composites of real situations, and any resemblance to people living or dead is coincidental.

Unless otherwise identified, all Scripture quotations in this publication are taken from the *New American Standard Bible* (NASB), © The Lockman Foundation 1960, 1962, 1963, 1968, 1971, 1972, 1973, 1975, 1977; Other versions used include the *HOLY BIBLE: NEW INTERNATIONAL VERSION®* (NIV®). Copyright © 1973, 1978, 1984 by International Bible Society. Used by permission of Zondervan Publishing House. All rights reserved; and the *New King James Version* (NKJV), copyright © 1979, 1980, 1982, 1990, Thomas Nelson Inc., Publishers.

Rinehart, Stacy.
        Upside down : the paradox of servant leadership / Stacy T. Rineheart.
             p. cm.
        Includes bibliographical references.
        ISBN 1-57683-079-9 (pbk.)
        1. Christian leadership. I. Title.
        BV652.1.R55 1998
        253—dc21
                                             98-10669
                                               CIP

Printed in the United States of America

7 8 9 10 11 12 13 14 / 15 14 13 12 11

To Paula, my wife and best friend.
With great love and patience she helped
me live and work out this book.

CONTENTS

FOREWORD

SPIRITUAL LEADERSHIP IN THE LATE TWENTIETH CENTURY FLOURISHES with entrepreneurial style. It typically focuses on the ministry of a single, strong individual. And that person is considered successful if he or she manages to gather a loyal following of people who organize to carry out this leader's goals.

Stacy Rinehart has another vision of spiritual leadership. The true spiritual leader, Stacy writes, is one who turns his or her focus away from self and the creation of a ministry empire in order to selflessly serve others and make them the heroes. Stacy takes his cues from the Bible, where he finds the most surprising leader of all time stating His grand objective: "I am the good shepherd; I know my sheep and my sheep know me—just as the Father knows me and I know the Father—and I lay down my life for the sheep" (John 10:14-15).

The Good Shepherd takes time to know His sheep, not as a general reviewing the ranks of his soldiers, not as a business manager reviewing the progress of his employees, but in the deepest intimacy, in just the same intimacy that He knows the Father.

Further, the Good Shepherd loves His sheep, loves them enough to joyfully lay down His own life for them. What an astonishing reversal of everything we see and hear in the church today!

The true spiritual leader observes with worship and awe the inner relations of the Trinity. He sees the *perichoresis*, or "mutual interpenetration at all points," of the Trinity as the model of loving relationships within the church. There should be no clergy/laity caste system like the one that has built up over the ages. Everyone is a leader in some realm, and all should submit to one another.

Dag Hammarskjöld once said that he learned this radical lesson from the Gospels: "All men are equals as God's children and should be met and treated by us as our masters." This is the lesson Stacy Rinehart wants us to learn in *Upside Down*. He turns the discipline of leadership upside down and shows us that "whoever wants to become great among you must be your servant" (Matthew 20:26).

This is radical thinking because the Bible is radical. The Word of God strikes at the roots of the hierarchical structures that have grown up like a choking undergrowth that stifles new life. What Stacy advocates (and what he has devoted his life to) is the development and release of people for ministry, according to thoroughly biblical principles. As Moses sought the release of the ancient people of Israel from soul-numbing slavery, Stacy wants to see the people of God released from false assumptions about who is qualified to perform ministry. Further, he wants to see each individual developed according to his or her gifting. Only then can each member of the body of believers enjoy a rightful destiny as an indispensable contributor to God's kingdom.

This vision for the individual is Stacy's passion. I have known him for over two decades, and we have worked together on innumerable projects in The Navigators. Most recently, we shared leadership in the task of creating the training program for the CoMission, a cooperative ministry of over eighty organizations that gathered to send several thousand lay missionaries to the former Soviet Union. In every instance, Stacy has shown self-giving deference to others and their opinions. And with utmost patience he has worked to support the unique contribution of every person involved.

The CoMission training project was mammoth, and Stacy put in eighteen-hour days for many months. He worked with a committee of over thirty individuals from diverse organizations. Invariably, I have heard these men and women remark on Stacy's leadership. They express what I have observed for all the years I have known him: He lives what he preaches.

Stacy is truly a servant leader. It is without reservation that I commend his book to you.

DR. TERRY TAYLOR
President, U.S. Navigators

PREFACE

Every book is written with a purpose in mind. First, I simply felt compelled to write and agonize over this topic. Over the last ten years I have been working at understanding leaders, ministry organizations, and spiritual leadership with a view to writing this book. I have collected over six feet of files, read hundreds of books, written thousands of notes, and had hundreds of in-depth conversations with leaders on this topic.

Second, I envision a massive movement of God's people, the laity, released and deeply involved in ministry. This movement is already happening, but there are indications that it is increasing in intensity. We have little hope of reaching our nation, or any nation, if the laity is not equipped and released for this God-mandated task. Leaders who do not serve the laity in this—those who strive to control lay ministry and want to keep the laity locked up under their "leadership"—may get run over! This book offers reasons for releasing serving leadership that will fan the enormous lay workforce in evangelism, outreach, missions, and ministry among the lost and the saved.

Third, I want to serve ministry leaders who are called to serve God's people. I have a deep love for these brothers and sisters who are called first as servants of Christ. I trust this book will encourage them in their basic calling to serve as Jesus did.

Leadership is a big topic. One cannot delve into this area on a whim and expect to master the field without many mentors, experiences, and much thought and study. And no one can write a book alone. This book has been over ten years in the making, and others have been teaching me about the subject of servant leadership for over twenty-five years.

My mentors in the faith have all taught me lessons for a lifetime. They are Chet Steffey, Gordon VanAmburgh, Elliott Johnson, Jim White, John Crawford, Skip Gray, Paul Stanley, Jim Petersen, Donald McGilchrist, and Terry Taylor. I am indebted to them for their investment in me.

Some have helped me in the areas of research, editing, typing, or just plain thinking, and so they are a part of the finished product, too. Notably, Rese Hood gave invaluable time to the original manuscript and has been a raving fan of the message of the book. Jeri McKee, Andria Wolfe, and Dennis Stokes have helped at various critical times. I don't know what I would have done without them.

I am committed to a community of brothers in Raleigh, and they to me. They, and their families, are all part of my community and are brothers who hold me up: Floyd Green, Bill Mann, Jim Anthony, Ralph Ennis, and more recently, Michael Mangum. At critical times, they also hold me in check. Frankly, I don't know how I could have gone through the process of life and ministry in the last seven years without these dear brothers. Their part in this process has been foundational.

One does not lead in a vacuum, nor have I practiced or refined the principles of this book by myself. I am indebted to my colleagues in The Navigators and my friends, colleagues, and partners in the CoMission who have encouraged me and believed in me for the message of this book.

Stacy T. Rinehart
Raleigh, North Carolina
September 1997

A NOTE TO THE READER

Who should read this book? It's intended for those who are Sunday school leaders and teachers, Bible study leaders, discipleship group leaders, pastors, church ministry staff members, elders, deacons, vestry members, church and ministry organization board members, missionaries, and ministry leaders. In short, this book is written for anyone trying to influence or lead others spiritually. If this list includes you, read on!

1

THE LEADERSHIP LADDER
Power: The Basis for Secular Leadership

FOR AS LONG AS I CAN REMEMBER, I'VE BEEN INTRIGUED WITH THE subject of leadership.

Whatever the setting—Boy Scouts, school, the army, business, the church—I saw *the leader* as being the most influential person. He was the one who got things done as he climbed the ladder of power.

My first significant experience in leadership came courtesy of McDonald's ™ in 1966. Fresh out of high school, I worked as an assistant manager in one of Ray Kroc's original restaurants in southern California. I channeled all my energies into the task of being the best up-and-coming manager. By day I helped manage a fast-paced business; at night I worked on a degree in business management.

My understanding of leadership at that time could have been summarized by a straightforward, unadorned idea: You're a leader when you're in charge, when people work for you and you call the shots. This was the code I lived by every day. A leader was the person who made it all happen. He played the fiddle to which others danced. Being the leader was perhaps the best hedge I knew against my fear of leading an inconsequential life.

I also developed a hard-nosed, aggressive style of motivating people, one that produced the most efficient results. In a business where quality, cleanliness, and speed are crucial, this style was rewarded and praised. I quickly became known as a manager who wouldn't let an employee get away with much. If someone didn't perform well, I let him or her go—as many as nine people in a single day! Somewhere in the back of my mind, though, I wondered whether there were better ways to influence people. So I turned to my studies all the more earnestly.

CLIMBING THE RIGHT LADDER?

In my business classes and textbooks, I hoped to encounter the model of truly effective leadership. I wanted something like a blueprint to manage and motivate people, and the business department of a university seemed to be the logical place to look. While my classes were stimulating, the foundational principle seemed quite similar to the one I applied every day on the hamburger line: A good leader is the guy who gets people to do what he wants done.

Before I could make progress in my studies, however, President Richard Nixon sent me a personal letter inviting me to take a free physical. Rather than take my chances on being drafted, I decided to enroll in the Army's Officer Candidate School. If I had to slog my way through the jungles of Vietnam, I at least wanted to be the one giving the orders.

In the army, the smoldering fire of my raw ambition burst into bold flame. We were instructed to keep our helmets polished to a mirror shine. On the inside of the helmet, right above our foreheads, we pinned the goal we were shooting for—a brass second lieutenant's bar. The next rung on the army officer's ladder must never be too far from his field of vision. I, however, was unwilling to stop with just a lieutenant's bar. I was the only man in my company who added the entire gamut of military brass inside my helmet liner—first lieutenant, captain, major, lieutenant colonel, colonel—all the way to four-star general.

I ran with the weight of enough bars and stars to break my neck.

While I had no intention of making a career of the army, I deeply subscribed to the basic philosophy of leadership it espoused. Whether military or civilian, being a leader was, in some way, a matter of climbing one's way up an invisible ladder to the top. There, at the top, the reward was power—power to make things happen, power to control the options, power to influence others.

If one metaphor for becoming a leader is climbing a ladder, then surely another is running a race. There are winners and losers in every race, and it's crucial not to be left behind. In the army we said it like this: Some helped you along, some stood in your way, and some waved as you passed by. I deeply wanted to be blazing a trail near the front.

I suppose I would have continued full speed ahead, except for one thing. The reality of death was beginning to stare me in the face. I was training as an infantry officer, and I knew I could easily be carried out of the jungle feet first. I had buddies just like me—young, ambitious, and full of life—who had left for Vietnam and come home in flag-draped coffins. Their funerals broke through my ambition and stripped me of my idealistic illusions. What difference would it make to rise to the top if what awaited me was only the cold, gray question mark of death?

I began reading the New Testament in search of answers.

Then one Saturday morning I found myself joining a "pick up" football game at Fort Benning, Georgia. This group of guys was just different enough to make me wonder what was up (the absence of obscenities was, in itself, noteworthy). They invited me that evening to a "party," and I arrived just in time for refreshments. After a while a helicopter pilot pulled me aside and shared the good news.

He explained that Christ's death made friends out of two enemies—God and me. The pilot said, "Stacy, becoming one of God's sons is a free gift—a gift that lasts for all eternity." It was an offer that sounded too good to be true as I recognized in the person of Jesus Christ the peace of mind that had long eluded me.

I began to read the Bible, but this time I read from the vantage point of one who had been introduced to its Author. The words took on great meaning, especially as I read the Gospels. There, Jesus the man came alive for me. I had never encountered anyone like Him. In particular, I was struck by His leadership style. Although He could have wielded His power to accomplish His aims, He chose not to do so. When Peter drew out his sword and cut off a soldier's ear, Christ rebuked him and healed the man who would carry Him into custody. I remember coming upon passages on leadership like the one in Mark 10. I'd never read anything like this in my business management books or in military leadership manuals:

> "You know that those who are recognized as rulers of the Gentiles lord it over them; and their great men exercise authority over them. But it is not so among you, but whoever wishes to become great among you shall be your servant; and whoever wishes to be first among you shall be slave of all." (Mark 10:42-44)

Immediately my interest was piqued. Here was Jesus addressing the issue of leadership directly, and I could hardly believe what I was reading. I found myself closing the Bible after reading verses like these and just shaking my head incredulously. The greatest leader was actually the greatest servant? Jesus contradicted everything I had thought, learned, and experienced concerning the subject of leadership. Leading from a position of authority and power might be the accepted way of the world, but Jesus said *it must not be so among His people.* His was a radically different approach.

SHIFTING FOUNDATIONS

When I was a boy, I loved to build. It didn't really matter what I built—tree houses, forts, or airplane models—as long as I was building. But very early I learned two important lessons. First, I saw that the foundations of any structure determine its effectiveness and stability. Second, to an uncanny degree, the final outcome reflects the model constructed in one's mind. Foundations, models, right beginnings—these matter more than they appear.

What I experienced as a young believer—that sense of shifting from one way of looking at leadership to favoring another approach—was once called a paradigm shift. A paradigm is our mental framework on a given topic or concern. It's our fundamental perspective, consisting of the guidelines, values, priorities, and sets of ideas we live by. These perspective patterns, or models, are incredibly powerful. They determine outcomes. Like the foundations of the structures I built as a child, they determine the beginning, the ending, and much that happens in between.

What happened to me was a foundational shift in the area of my greatest interest—leadership. When I read that John and James had unabashedly asked Jesus for the top posts in His kingdom, I wasn't surprised; that's what I would have done. It's what any smart opportunist would do. I knew that the other disciples were angry only because it left them further back in the line. John and James had simply seized the opportunity first. That longing to be first was something I understood well. But I saw, too, that Christ immediately described a whole other way to be first, one I had never seriously considered. His fundamental criterion for being "first" in the kingdom was to be a servant. *Servanthood* was the Savior's measure of determining greatness.

Naturally, my own leadership practices came into question as I encountered Scripture. Almost immediately I began a process of reevaluation. As a new believer, I had a sense of starting over on many fronts, and nowhere was this more true than in my ambition and attitudes as a leader. Suddenly the stars and bars in my helmet liner seemed terribly out of place. I realized I had climbed *the wrong leadership ladder.* I was scaling the wrong wall.

I cringed as I thought of all the people I had summarily dismissed. And what opportunities I had missed to serve people! The more I read the Bible, the more I sensed the close connection between failing to serve and failing to lead.

I had so much to learn.

LEANING THE LADDER ON A NEW WALL

My conviction that Jesus lived and taught a different model of leadership from the world's has only deepened through the years. Yet tactics typified by dominance, rank, positional authority, and turf protection do seem to be effective in the short run.

Just yesterday my close friend and colleague, Dennis Stokes, and I spent an hour perusing a nearby book superstore, looking at the self-help books and the business books. In the business section alone there were ten bookcases with eight shelves each — eighty shelves of business books. In the first several shelves, here were some of the book titles:

- *Reengineering Yourself*
- *Mary Kay: You Can Have It All*
- *Sex, Money & Power*
- *The New Professional Image*

These books seemed to have a definite theme. Then Dennis and I looked through the self-help shelves and found these titles:

- Best seller *Unlimited Power* by Anthony Robbins (1986).
- *Awaken the Giant Within* by Anthony Robbins (1991). This book uses Matthew 7:7 on page 163 to encourage getting what you want.
- *Manifest Your Destiny* by Dr. Wayne Dyer (1997). On the cover it says, "The Nine Spiritual Principles for Getting Everything You Want."
- Best seller *Getting to Yes* by Roger Fisher and William Ury (1991).

Through our culture, we are getting a "spiritual" message from many directions. Thought-shaping books are just one medium. Yet, if adapted with spiritual terminology, they take the life out of our ministries. In the long run, both leaders and followers burn out under these approaches.

Leading as the world leads — through manipulation, personal

charisma, or subtle intimidation—dies hard in each of us as believers. It's the model we've most often seen and experienced, and we want to keep climbing the ladder of power and authority. All too often, when people come close to the center of the action in churches and religious organizations, they find that our ways of relating to each other—our leadership practices—differ only slightly from those in the boardroom of any corporation.

In effect, we have leaned our leadership ladder on the shifting, tottering wall of secular leadership theories and practices. We need a new wall to lean on, a new model of leadership that flows from biblical principles.

What would happen if we lifted the lid on the average church or ministry organization today? Would we not, in many cases, find a detailed study in the use of ego, power, and control perfected to an art form? In a strange way, the misuse of power seems to flourish in religious institutions. Here human ambition can become coated with the veneer of spirituality. As a result, we fail to ask ourselves the hard questions. Our spiritual position in the community of faith becomes the curtain behind which our egos grow unchecked. The younger ones in the faith dare not question us—the spiritual elders. And we grow more and more skilled at covering up our insecurities.

All too often, when people come close to the center of the action in churches and religious organizations, they find that our ways of relating to each other—our leadership practices—differ only slightly from those in the boardroom of any corporation.

Staggering as it may seem, Jesus' main opposition came from powerful religious leaders. Is it any different in our day? A close look at the Gospels reveals that in Jesus' day the only institution He confronted was the religious one. He bypassed the Roman government and overlooked the local magistrates. It was the scribes and Pharisees He took on directly.

Woe to you, He said, because you have become a barrier, not a bridge, to people in search of God. He labeled them "blind guides" who strained to perfect their image—"the outside of the cup"—while neglecting the hidden grime on the inside. They were leaders who majored on their own images and minored on substance and truth. And it's deeply sobering to realize that the religious rather than the secular leaders arranged Christ's death.

I now realize that God was beginning the process of turning my head and heart upside down about what it means to lead people well. That experience has been a slow, soul-searching one, extending over twenty years of leading.

Leadership is a topic that spills over into so many areas of life because it is fundamental to both how we treat each other and how we perceive ourselves. Leadership—or what has historically constituted leadership—is also a burning issue for the body of Christ today. I believe that if we were pressed to answer the question, "What holds the church back?" many of us would answer from some deep, sober corner of our soul: *Her leaders.* Far too often the church's leaders have been and are the bottleneck in the system.

Our Christian leaders often take up the "power leadership" practices of the world around us. This perspective has crept in to deny true servanthood, yet we've accepted it. In copying the strategies and principles of secular leadership, we thwart the work of God in people's lives and become not servants but a hindrance to the very ministry we want to happen.

This book is a call to reexamine our most basic models of leadership in ministry. Together we will try to answer the question of what constitutes true leadership—*spiritual* leadership. My deep conviction is that there's a true difference between the leadership principles Christ taught and those that typically hold sway in our ministries.

But the process of returning to God's fundamental concepts of spiritual leadership takes time and care. This book is not for the insecure or fainthearted. It is not intended to make you comfortable, especially if you're content with the status quo of leadership in your ministry or if you've been unwilling to take a realistic look at how you've led so far. Indeed, we'll expose some critical issues. But it's well worth the effort. Ministries will come alive once again, and people will find renewed joy in service. And, best of all, God will be glorified.

■
□

REFLECT ON YOUR LEADERSHIP

- Consider your current leadership philosophy. What are your major premises and assumptions? From where have your leadership models and practices come? How are they similar to and different from models and practices in the business world?
- Who are some of your leadership heroes? What qualities do they possess? To what extent have you emulated these people?
- How have the Scriptures moderated or changed your leadership views and actions over the years?
- Have you ever lost the opportunity to serve someone because of your leadership style? What happened?

Respond to the Challenge

Beware of the temptation to lean your "leadership ladder" against the wall of purely secular models and practices.

■ ■ ■

Lord, please help me to recognize where I have accepted a secular power model of leadership that is contrary to Your will.

2

NOT SO AMONG YOU

Servanthood: The Essence of Spiritual Leadership

HAD BEEN IN FULL-TIME MINISTRY WITH THE NAVIGATORS FOR A FEW
years and was facing a number of leadership issues that come
with any ministry, so I determined to attend a conference enti-
tled "Leadership in the Church." The week-long series of work-
shops featured a prominent professor from a leading seminary. I
arrived with great anticipation, looking forward to new ideas and
fresh insights. This was my chance to rub shoulders with ministry peers from churches and other ministry organizations and to
learn from the experts.

Alas! For a whole week we received nothing but basic management principles derived from the business and military arenas.
I'd heard it all before. This time, however, the same ideas were
coated with enough spiritual veneer to camouflage their source.

There must be more to the topic of spiritual leadership than
just attaching a Scripture reference to secular management principles. Do we, as kingdom citizens, have something unique to
offer on this subject—something as profoundly different as what
we see modeled in the relationships within the Trinity and the early
church? Or is Christ's teaching about servant leadership just a
nice addendum to our already crowded leadership ideals?

A Fork in the Road

What I observed in that week-long conference has become a disturbing trend over the years. We are currently running unchecked toward a wholesale acceptance of secular business models in our concepts of leadership and structures.

The more modern and sophisticated we become, the greater our tendency to take on the world's basic management philosophies to accomplish kingdom work. It's as though we believe, deep down, that Christ's teaching on servant leadership is an anachronism, better left to the dusty roads of Galilee with its ox-drawn carts. How could such leadership apply to our busy, pressure-filled age? Yet, the apostle Paul warned against this tendency: "See to it that no one takes you captive through philosophy and empty deception, according to the tradition of men, according to the elementary principles of the world, rather than according to Christ" (Colossians 2:8).

Servant leadership is not an impossible ideal in our day. Rather, it should be the foundational cornerstone of our thinking about spiritual leadership. Christ lived, taught, and modeled it for us, and it is our true distinctive as believers.

We are meant to relate to each other in ways the world would like to emulate. But apart from the indwelling Holy Spirit, it is impossible. So rather than take our cues from the culture around us, we ought to capitalize on what makes spiritual leadership truly kingdom focused: "a leadership which is not modeled on the power games of the world, but on the servant leader, Jesus, who came to give His life for the salvation of many."[1]

Do you remember Christ's encounter with James and John, when they asked Him for seats of honor and privilege beside Him? It's truly a pivotal passage on leadership.

In many ways, the attitude of these two disciples effectively summarizes the prevailing attitude about leadership, one that reasserts itself with every generation. The "lords of the Gentiles"—the power leaders—naturally seek a rank above others. Human nature looks for the shortest path to the top, the most self-gratifying position, regardless of the cost to others. The leader gets to call the shots from his position of power and control. James and John recognized this, and having seen that Christ could put them in a place of honor if He chose, they asked Him to make them leaders.

I find it interesting that Jesus never reprimanded His disciples for wanting "to be great." Instead He dramatically redefined the terms of greatness and pointed His disciples in another direction entirely. You can be leaders, He told them, but you must take the route of sacrifice, suffering, and service. "Whoever wants to become great among you must be your servant, and whoever wants to be first must be slave of all" (Mark 10:43-44).

This classic passage in Mark brings us to a fork in the road called leadership. The fork gives us two distinct directions, or models, and each will lead us to entirely different outcomes. One route relies on power, authority, and control. The other path — the one that follows in Christ's footsteps, however imperfectly — is a road of humility and of putting others first. In other words, Jesus cut through the superfluous issues surrounding leadership and moved straight to the heart of the matter. His words address our motives and values.

Thus, we are drawn to consider the unseen realities from which we move into others' lives. Each of us has a mental model of leadership, and that model defines how we operate, how we go about ministry. The model is constructed from more than our church traditions or the particular branch of theology we represent. A leadership model that rests on the power inherent in the position will eventually hinder the task of releasing and empowering others for ministry. A servant leadership model, on the other hand, helps equip and liberate others to fulfill God's purposes for them in the world. As such, our leadership models are crucially important.

Let's examine more closely the role of values, assumptions, and principles as they relate to our leadership models.

VALUES, ASSUMPTIONS, AND PRINCIPLES

All of life rests on three words. If I sit down and prop up my feet in my favorite easy chair, it's because I have a *value:* Rest is a good thing. As I choose that chair and move toward it, I am making an *assumption:* This will support my weight. The fact that both the chair and I remain grounded and in one place is due to some basic *principles* of gravity and physics.

In the same way, the leadership models from which we operate are rooted in particular values, assumptions, and principles. They are the invisible, but determinative, core beliefs that govern what we do and how we relate. *Not until we have considered our leadership model at the level of its values, assumptions, and principles, can we discern to what extent we are leading from a power or a servant base.* This is why looking beneath the surface of our activities and experiences as leaders is so important. Our core beliefs about leadership will determine whether a power or servant leadership model prevails.

When I give a leadership seminar, I usually carve out a slice of time in which, as a group, we analyze the prevailing philosophies and practices that business and military leaders currently espouse. We look at advice and instruction flowing from leading secular experts. Here are some of the questions we ask:

- What basic values about people and tasks are driving this leadership philosophy?
- What are the assumptions about the leader's role and the role of those *not* called "leaders"?
- To what authoritative principles does the leader subscribe?
- What qualities are applauded in this leadership model?

After analyzing prevailing leadership trends at the level of values, assumptions, and operative principles, we then compare them with definitions of leadership typically offered from a ministry perspective. Over and over again, groups reach this conclusion: There is little difference in the management philosophy of either camp. Whether the spokesperson is a leader in the church or in a corporate setting, much of the basic mantra is the same. As a quick example, read the following definitions of leadership and decide which comes from a secular book and which is a definition from a well-known Christian author:

- [Here is] one of the most straightforward definitions of leadership we have found: "In essence, leadership appears to be the art of getting others to want to do something you are convinced should be done." Two words in this definition stand out as most significant: to want. Without "to want" in the definition, the meaning of leadership is significantly altered. Choice, internal motivation, and inner desire disappear. Leadership then implies force or something less than voluntary involvement.[2]

- The concept of leadership in this book means one who guides activities of others and who himself acts and performs to bring those activities about. He is capable of performing acts which will guide a group in achieving objectives. He takes the capacities of vision and faith, has the ability to be concerned and to comprehend, and exercises action through effective and personal influence in the direction of an enterprise and the development of the potential into the practical and/or profitable means. To accomplish this, a true leader must have a strong drive to take the initiative to act—a kind of initial stirring that causes people and an organization to use their best abilities to accomplish a desired end.[3]

Tough to decide? Whether the topic is goal setting, delegation, effective management, motivation, or effecting change, evangelical and secular authors seem to present a common leadership philosophy. As Dr. David McKenna has stated,

Another approach in the search for distinctive Christian leadership is to begin with the premises of secular leadership theory and raise them to a spiritual level with an overlay of biblical principles. . . . The weakness is the starting point. By beginning with the premises of secular leadership theory, the assumptions underlying the theory are also accepted. Without a critique of those assumptions, which invariably influence the motive and mission of leadership, conflicts will arise when biblical and secular assumptions clash in practice.[4]

This disturbing trend has been around a long time, as observed and lamented by many writers and leaders. Almost twenty years ago, organizational consultant Myron Rush said, "It is tragic that so many Christian organizations have accepted the world's philosophy of management. They [attempt] to accomplish God's work using a management philosophy diametrically opposed to biblical principles."[5]

Yet, sometimes we don't immediately discern this opposition to God's principles until we begin to apply the philosophies and observe their damaging effects. In the 1960s, for example, "management by objectives" (MBO) became popular and was adopted by many Christian organizations. Leaders discovered Scripture verses that seemed to support this pragmatic concept. If it worked for the world, it must work for Christians, too, especially if we found a biblical rationale.

This MBO philosophy led to clear goal statements and workable systems, profiles, standards, and tools for evaluation. Yet it became easy to over-analyze, over-specify, and over-inspect. Recently, a ministry leader wrote to me with this confession:

Early in my ministry I, too, was fooled by the seeming rightness of this approach for a while. My motives were to accomplish God's work and to produce as much as possible for His kingdom. And yet things sometimes turned sour. People around me felt like objects being manipulated.

"The Goal Rules" took precedence over "The Golden Rule." I began drawing small, arbitrary boxes to put people into. If they didn't conform, they didn't fit. The systems were often well organized and elaborate — and expected things not found in God's Word. Furthermore, God Himself was often left out of these formulas. A few of the people around me felt used, abused, and forced into these unrealistically created molds. This approach made it

too easy to depend on self and not God, to fulfill my
objectives and not God's. But the fallacy of this approach
was deceiving.

Eventually I went to the individuals I had abused, at
least the ones I knew about, and asked their forgiveness.
And at one ministry reunion a number of years ago, I apol-
ogized on my behalf and on behalf of my organization.

Actually, it seemed logical and natural to use the MBO
approach then. Today we continue the trend of looking to the
business culture for our leadership concepts and practices. Only
today, the terms are different such as: consensus, flattening the
organization, quality control, and so forth. This method empha-
sizes the truth and warning of Colossians 2:8: "See to it that no
one takes you captive through hollow and deceptive philosophy,
which depends on human tradition and the basic principles of
this world rather than on Christ." Here we are warned against
three things and commended to only one:

Warning: against "hollow and deceptive philosophy"
(*Not* rationalism—the world or my mind decides what is right)

Warning: against "human tradition"
(*Not* traditionalism—the way we or others did it before is right)

Warning: against "basic principles of this world"
(*Not* pragmatism—if it works it must be right)

Affirmation: "Rather . . . on Christ"
(*Dependence*—*His wisdom and strength make things work out right*)

In his book on servant leadership, Paul Cedar, chairman of Mission America, warned leaders to be on guard:

As servant leaders we will soon discover that we are
swimming against the stream. The concepts of servant
leadership are contrary to much of what most of us have

learned about leadership and management from such highly respected sources. As we explore servant leadership from a biblical perspective, we will find that it is "out of tune" with much of the most highly respected management systems popular today.[6]

It's likely that leaders who accomplish their goals by power, position, and authority are easier to live with in the corporate setting than in the church. In a ministry setting, a leader who so chooses can use guilt and shame to an uncanny degree. In the church, the playing field is never level if the leader sets himself up as the one who speaks for God. Who would dare question "God"? At least the business world doesn't add that spiritual confusion.

THE POWER LEADERSHIP MODEL

I'm not saying that secular leadership philosophies offer us nothing of value. But we appear to have adopted many of them wholesale, without significant critique. Prayerful, reflective analysis has fallen by the wayside. We will always fall easy prey to the latest, most popular trends if we fail to consider our leadership models at the level of values and assumptions. When we do look at the basic values of "power leadership" in the church and paint them in broad brush strokes, we find at least five driving values that have remained constant over the last several decades.

Standardization
This value assumes that sameness and uniformity can be achieved. The basic idea is that when people do the ministry in the same way and in the same manner, everything as a result will move forward. Standardization influences our ministry practices when it determines how we do evangelism or run a Sunday school. It can dictate the path of growth that every believer, ministry, or church needs to trod in order to reach maturity. It ignores the variety of creative ways God might choose to do things.

When standardization infiltrates a ministry program, the results are then viewed as contingent upon how well everyone carries out a preordained method. Doing it *the same way* becomes the prerequisite for success. Here's the assumption: If ministry formulas and activities are reproduced accurately from place to place, in each life, from one year to the next, then spiritual success will result.

Conformity

During a seminar, I once asked, "How would you define the ideal Christian?" I was amazed at how quickly people responded, speaking in terms of one's devotional life, evangelism habits, monetary giving patterns, church involvement, and family life. From group to group, as I've asked that question, I've received strikingly similar responses. *Doing* is deemed more important in our ministries than *being*. Yet this outlook negates a sense of God's dealing in each person's inner life in unique ways. Nevertheless, actions are easy to replicate, and the degree of consensus can be measured and evaluated. By focusing on outward appearances we can quickly tell how spiritual we are.

Of course, if our unconscious goal is conformity, then—as leaders—we will push our ministries toward that end. We will work to inject one ingredient here and another there in assembly-line fashion, all in the impossible pursuit of producing the ideal, complete believer.

Pragmatism

Seminars offering the latest techniques for growing a church often feature "CEO pastors" or business leaders who have succeeded in *producing* a large ministry. One question is basic to pragmatism. How did it happen? How does it work? How can we get this to happen too? The assumption is: "If it works, it must be good." When *how* is the central question, the Bible becomes a secondary authority and *what works* becomes the primary value.

Does the end always justify the means?

Pure pragmatism is a close cousin to moral relativism. If what works determines what we do, when something no longer works we're forced to find some other way to get things done. In other words, the end justifies the means, regardless of whether the means are right or wrong. If we follow the path of least cultural resistance, we'll find ourselves heading down a trail that leads away from the Scriptures.

Productivity

In our culture, producing is the bottom line. If you don't *produce,* you will be asked to leave. It's true in business, and it's often the case in our churches and ministries. As long as our ministry is growing rapidly, everything seems fine. Members overlook obvious problems in the leader's life, family, or ministry, as long as he or she continues to bring in the people who keep it all going. When production is the overriding value, we often neglect to ask the hard questions. After all, who's going to argue with success?

Today, personal worth is measured by the ability to produce. We esteem the pastor of a large church more than the pastor of a small one. We seek to emulate the ministry with the greatest statistical growth. As in the business world, production is the guiding light. Unfortunately, this engenders competition among ministries, pitting them against one another. The net effect is not unity in the body of Christ.

Centralization

Power leadership holds that someone must be in control; someone must account for the bottom line. In the words of Peter Block, "It's almost a religious belief that control must come from the top and from outside ourselves for us to operate in a way that we are comfortable." He also points out that "the strongest wish of the organization is to maintain control at all costs, and this is the single most dominant value in pyramidal organizations."[7]

Centralization assumes that a leader speaks for God and that people are there to support the leader's vision of what needs to be accomplished. *Following along* with the leader or organization becomes a basic tenet of godliness. Failing to submit is to rebel against God Himself!

These five driving values of power systems—standardization, conformity, pragmatism, productivity, and centralization—often lead to abusive leadership behavior. Followers become tools that leaders use to accomplish laudable ends. In this way, people have worth to the leader and his system only as long as they participate dutifully without rocking the boat. As Alister McGrath explains in his book *Power Religion,*

> There are remarkable, and disturbing, parallels between the distorted idea of priesthood in the medieval church and the notion of ministry found within modern power evangelicalism. Both are intensely authoritarian. Both rest upon an ideology of power, which places the right to speak for God in the hands of a small and unaccountable elite. Both studiously ignore the possibility that they might get God wrong, and the deeply threatening and humiliating possibility that God might choose to challenge and correct them through ordinary lay folk within their undervalued congregations.[8]

THE SERVANT LEADERSHIP MODEL

God calls us to another kind of leadership among His people — an approach in which leaders exist in order to serve. We don't naturally gravitate to this type of leadership, but it happens when we give up our own interests to genuinely look out for the well-being of those we are called to serve. An entirely different set of assumptions undergirds this model, as well as a different source of power. Philip Greenslade put it nicely: "In a radical fashion, Jesus, by example and word, establishes servanthood as the way in which his men are to lead others. He expressly repudiates every secular model of leadership in favor of servanthood."[9]

Let's take a closer look at what Jesus and His apostles said about leadership:

- "And do not be called leaders; for One is your Leader, *that is,* Christ." (Matthew 23:10)
- "But the greatest among you shall be your servant." (Matthew 23:11)

- "And whoever exalts himself shall be humbled; and whoever humbles himself shall be exalted." (Matthew 23:12)
- Not that we lord it over your faith, but are workers with you for your joy; for in your faith you are standing firm. (2 Corinthians 1:24)
- For we do not preach ourselves but Christ Jesus as Lord, and ourselves as your bond-servants for Jesus' sake. (2 Corinthians 4:5)
- Nor yet as lording it over those allotted to your charge, but proving to be examples to the flock. (1 Peter 5:3)

These verses reflect a different set of values from the prevailing mental model of leadership; they spring from God's Word. Servant leadership springs from a set of values, assumptions, and principles that counter those of the secular world. We might bring out the contrast by juxtaposing standardization, conformity, pragmatism, and control through productivity with diversity, empowerment, dependence on the Scriptures, and authenticity.

Diversity Instead of Standardization

Standardization stifles freedom and demotivates people—especially those who are creative. Highly gifted people often avoid standardized ministries because of the pressure to conform.

Servant leadership allows freedom to vary methods, styles, forms, and visions because the diversity of the body is valued. The resulting ministry will continually adjust, adapt, and invent new approaches as gifted people move away from standardized values, expectations, and assumptions. Here, the power of God's Spirit flourishes.

Jesus never evangelized the same way twice. He told Nicodemus he must be born again. From the Samaritan woman, he asked for a drink of water, then launched into a dialogue with her. To a crippled and disabled man he said, "Do you wish to get well?" (John 5:6). Jesus did not use standardized methods; rather, He fit His approach to individual needs and personalities.

Empowerment, Not Conformity

Conformity treats all believers alike and expects them to *be* and *act* alike. Unique gifts are neither recognized nor valued. This retards the growth of the believer and the maturing of the local fellowship.

In contrast, servant leaders *equip* and *develop* people in ways that empower and release them to live according to their gifting and God-given calling. Individuals experience great freedom in the Spirit, as their contribution to the body is expected to be unlike anyone else's.

Consider Jesus and the twelve men He chose to be with Him. They were as diverse as any twelve Jews could be. Some were hyper-conservative — zealously propagating nationalism. Others were considered traitors to their own country—collecting taxes for the occupying Romans. The spectrum was as broad as it could be. Yet no conformity was required, though the potential for internal conflict within the group was high. The Twelve chose to follow Jesus, not because they were manipulated into being like Him, but because of the compelling quality of His character.

Centered in the Scriptures Rather than Pragmatism

Pragmatism produces ministry technicians who rely on natural processes for empowerment. It is because we worship at the feet of this idol — pragmatism — that we so readily embrace business models. When the Bible is allowed to speak to the questions at hand, fresh approaches emerge. We begin to experience freedom to ask hard questions. We reassess our ministry practices as the Scriptures become truly authoritative for us. Sensitive to human needs and open to the Spirit's guidance, the servant leader directs people to the Scriptures. All ask together: How does God's Word address the issues at hand?

Too often in our day we fail to look to the Scriptures as an authority by itself. We quickly run to other sources for our answers: psychology, sociology, pragmatism, celebrities, the experts, business books and seminars, the latest Christian book on the subject, marketing strategies, mega-church leaders.

These become our *practical* authorities.

A servant leader, on the other hand, brings people back to the Bible. Doing what is right and true governs, not merely doing what works. Pragmatism alone will not produce lasting spiritual results.

Authenticity Above Productivity and Control

Production measures the externals, the visible results. It teaches people to live on an earthly plane and strive for certain appearances. It produces a kind of materialism in which more bodies, bigger buildings, and higher budgets predominate—all of which are justified under various religious terms and labels. The principles of the kingdom often are ignored.

> *A friend of mine once asked a pastor: "What would this church be like if it was built on your devotion to Christ rather than on your drive for a bigger and better church?" The pastor stared back, dumbfounded.*

The servant leader assumes that God has a different standard of evaluation for each person and ministry. It is God alone who produces fruit; we are fellow workers with Him in His harvest. His fruit is often hidden and always defies measurement. He uses different people in different ways through different processes. The value of authenticity allows people the freedom to do things in ministry that may seem to fail in the short run. But failure in our eyes may not be failure in God's eyes at all.

A friend of mine once asked a pastor: "What would this church be like if it was built on your devotion to Christ rather than on your drive for a bigger and better church?" The pastor stared back, dumbfounded.

I can only hope that he began to deal with his lack of authenticity. Placing importance on authenticity helps us to value what is real and lasting and to value the substance over the image. The fruit of the Spirit—the inner changes in people's lives—may be less measurable, yet they are no less genuine. Authenticity is, in fact, refreshing. It eliminates the games we play for show, removing the barriers to true relationship.

ASKING THE BIG QUESTION: WHY?

Although power and servant leadership models are essentially opposites, none of us lives totally in either camp. It will always be tempting to rely on some subtle form of power or manipulation to advance our own ends. We're constantly pulled in that direction as a kind of default position of our fallen human nature.

Yet, knowing the pull of our nature doesn't lessen the reality that God has given us a standard of servant leadership to embrace. He holds us accountable to the way of His Son. As such, the truth that He lives in me and in you is the encouragement that keeps us going in the right direction. Being a servant leader is not a type of internship we fulfill (in which we serve our time and then graduate into a place where we become the central figure — "the leader"). Jesus' graduation exercise was death. Servant leadership is, therefore, a lifelong, ongoing commitment. It lasts as long as God gives us people to shepherd in His care.

If this is the case, then we must periodically ask ourselves, "Why am I doing this?" At each juncture in the ministry, in the nitty-gritty of everyday tasks and encounters, we must allow this question to reassert itself: *Why am I doing this?* If we're willing to face our deepest motivations, we'll come to know those places in our lives in which we are controlled by our need to control. Asking the hard questions helps us recognize where power leadership has been the means by which we've gone about God's business.

Actually, *servant leadership* is a popular term today in both the business and power-oriented ministry worlds. But often those who speak and write about it focus on the second word: servant *leadership*. Viewed with this emphasis, serving is simply a means to an end: "I'll serve you, so you'll respect my leadership and follow me. I prime the pump, so you will deliver." This is just another subtle form of power leadership.

In *servant* leadership, serving is the expression of leadership, regardless of how people follow. Serving is both the end as well as the means. But it's not easy to lead in this way. The pressure to rely on power and control increases as the needs around us multiply. The urgency of the moment seems to justify any means at our disposal.

Nevertheless, we can resist this pressure to perform. We can stop and evaluate our methods. After all, the truest weapons available for our kingdom battles are faith, prayer, and dependence upon God and His people. Humble servants of the Lord's servants—those who follow Christ's example—win the real and lasting victories.

◼

REFLECT ON YOUR LEADERSHIP

- You've surveyed two different models of leadership in this chapter—power leadership and servant leadership. Describe each in your own words. Think of situations in which you've seen both models at work. What ministry leaders come to mind?
- Do you agree that we are "running unchecked toward a wholesale acceptance of the business models in our concepts of leadership and structures"? If this is true, what are some of the negative consequences of this trend?
- To what extent have you, or those in the ministry with which you are affiliated, examined the values, assumptions, and principles of leadership? What have you discovered?
- How have you heard the term *servant leadership* used in the past? Where has the emphasis been placed—on *servant* or on *leadership*? What practical consequences spring from the different emphases? Reflecting on your own ministry, what has been your emphasis?

Respond to the Challenge

Be willing to evaluate the leadership model from which you minister—especially considering its foundational values, assumptions, and principles.

■ ■ ■

I acknowledge to You, my Lord, that Your servant foundations are the only ones worthy for me to rely upon.

THE DARK SIDE OF LEADERSHIP
The Uses and Abuses of Power

IN HOPES OF DISCREDITING AN UPSTART GALILEAN PREACHER, THE Sanhedrin picked their most clever men to tail Him and investigate His ministry. What they saw was quite spectacular: lepers with baby-fresh skin; well-fed multitudes carrying baskets of picnic leftovers; a blind man exulting in the beauty of trees and clouds; a former demoniac clothed and sane; even a "dead" man walking through town.

But, of course, the people hounding Jesus were looking for other things.

FIXATED ON EXTERNALS

Jesus' ministry and miracles should have inspired a glorious praise and worship service at the temple. Instead, there was only suspicion, paranoia, and finally, murder. The religious elite felt deeply threatened. This strange man preached forgiveness apart from scrupulous adherence to the Law. Where did that leave *them*?

The religious system that developed in Israel after the

Babylonian captivity and through subsequent conquests had become the only means through which the people of Israel were taught they could reach God. This placed enormous power in the hands of a few men. Taking a cue from the Roman world in which they lived, they handled Jesus like any Roman would handle a traitor to their system—they had Him killed. Their system—fixated on external observances and appearances—had to be preserved at any cost.

Like the Sanhedrin of Jesus' day, much of what ministry leaders today believe and do in the realm of power, authority, and control has been borrowed not from Scriptures, but from the surrounding power institutions. Historically, we have confused institutional authority with spiritual authority. By blending the two together we can make them appear synonymous.

Henri Nouwen has said,

> One of the greatest ironies of the history of Christianity is that its leaders constantly gave in to the temptation of power—political power, military power, economic power, moral and spiritual power—even though they continued to speak in the name of Jesus, who did not cling to His divine power but emptied Himself and became as we are.[1]

Here's the reality: There is an epidemic of power leadership loose in churches and ministry organizations today. Power leaders are so common that we've lost our immunity to this style of leadership. The goal of this chapter is to identify some common misconceptions we hold about power, authority, and control.

All of us who share the human condition struggle with the temptations of power. A close friend of mine shared this story of his own struggle in one of his first official ministry roles:

> Here I was—a newly appointed staff person in my organization. For a long time I had wanted God to use my life, and now I had been given a clear position to lead. It was encouraging to have the respect of people from the start and have them looking to me for help. And God soon

provided a very gifted team of lay people to work with me. Even as a noncontrolling type person, I now faced new struggles since I had such a clear platform. I found myself very much desiring to have the *image* of the leader. I wanted to take the lead in almost every area, even if I was not as qualified as others on the team. I wanted to do the teaching, set the ministry focus, develop the strategies. After all, I was the full-time staff person. I really didn't want others to excel beyond me. I had to stay in front of them. Part of this was my own desire to control and maintain my image; part of it was my perception of a leader as one who does it all.

As time passed, I noticed discontent and frustration among some of the team members. They wanted to teach and lead but felt that I was locking up the limelight. Some folks moved on to other ministry involvements. One person told me he left primarily because of my overcontrol. Was that ever hard to hear! Others, too, were hurt by decisions I'd made *for* people more than *with* people.

I also created many expectations for how people should function—what they ought to do in their spiritual lives and what activities they should take up. We set up many hoops for people to jump through if they really wanted to be part of the group. Some left embittered because they felt a lack of acceptance and couldn't live up to our standards of conformity.

Through some of the Lord's painful ways of working within me, I realized I was selfishly hanging on to my own image, authority, and desire to control things and people. The bad news is that I had not yielded it to the Lord, and it had harmful effects on others. I began learning that I had gone too far in telling those around me how to live their lives. In setting standards for them that went beyond what God's Word specified, I caused a lot of grief. It was truly sin on my part.

The good news is that God chopped away this

cancerous growth and gave me grace to allow others on that team to teach and lead. Some went far beyond what I could have done. God also helped me release my controlling standards so others had more freedom. And He's still working on me.

POWER AND THE CHURCH

The reality of the struggle demands that we take a deeper look at the problem. Indeed, for each of us, a crucial step toward rediscovering the roots of spiritual leadership is to hack away some of the undergrowth obscuring it. Let's begin with a look at power in the church both yesterday and today.

In the Early Church

To a first-century believer, our customary question of "Who's in charge here?" would be met with a puzzled look. Members of the early church just didn't ask that question because their teachings centered on serving Christ and one another. A servant isn't accustomed to seeing himself as *in charge*.

At the core of Christ's own servant model of leadership was the giving up of one's life on behalf of others. Certainly His crucifixion was the supreme illustration, and this same kind of selflessness characterized the leadership of the first-century church. Nowhere was true spiritual maturity more evident than in times of persecution. To lead meant to flirt with sudden death, for leaders were the ones dragged before the authorities and murdered in an attempt to stifle the new "religious cult." Yet it was the desire to serve the people of God, not the quest for power or control, that moved the early disciples to persevere through trials, prison terms, and stonings.

Even a cursory glance at Scripture or the writings of first-century historian Josephus or even the legal record of Rome testifies that worldly power held by Christians in the first two centuries was very limited. Dogged by waves of persecution and shunned by both Gentiles and Jews, they spent their time serving spiritual, emotional, and physical needs.

This still holds true today in portions of the world where following Jesus is outlawed. On my first trip to the former Soviet Union, I talked with a sixty-year-old servant of Christ who served Jesus as an itinerant pastor in the Republic of Byelorussia. He and another pastor served an area roughly equivalent in size to the state of Colorado. Before each long trip, he would kiss his family good-bye, not knowing whether he'd ever return home again.

Before the fall of communism, the KGB targeted people who represented religious propagation, and this man was constantly harassed. He has since learned that his house was bugged in every room except the bathroom. Whenever he went on a trip, the KGB knew where he was going, when he would be there, how long he would stay, and when he would return. He was under constant surveillance. He still marvels that he was not killed or imprisoned.

Christ and the early church members modeled such risky servant leadership—risking and giving for something greater than themselves. Serving others in the service of the King and His kingdom was paramount.

When the apostle Paul pointed to a model of leadership to emulate, he chose two men. He chose them not for their splendid oration or competent managerial skills, but for their selflessness. Timothy was known for his genuine interest in people (see Philippians 2:20), and Epaphroditus "almost died for the work of Christ, risking his life. . . ."(Philippians 2:30).

In the Church Today
Our culture has become increasingly obsessed with the quest for power. Power lies in visibility and a carefully crafted image. As the saying goes, "Appearance is everything." Substance takes second place. To get ahead you have to push yourself past the next guy. I've seen it firsthand at ministry leadership conferences. We jockey for position even there, using subtle, ingenious tactics to figure out where everybody stands in the power-and-success lineup. The church is, in effect, a power advocate.

Power has become a familiar word in Christian circles.
Unlike the small church down the street we used to go to,

the new megachurch in a neighboring town has *powerful programs,* and its buildings often compete with corporate office buildings for the impressive architecture of power. Or, the healing service last week was *powerful:* we all felt the power. Or, we hear . . . "We are really gaining power in Washington. We're a powerful voting block."[2]

The issue is not megachurch *versus* small church, healing, *or* political activism. Rather, the issue is that we've adopted a secular view regarding what it takes to be an effective entity in the world—namely, a power that can be touched, tabulated, and made tangible. Yet it is a power at odds with the mystery of the mustard seed and the grain of salt—a resurrection power so vital and alive that it can operate out of sight in small, quiet, but truly unassailable ways.

Power, authority, and control manifest themselves in specific ways within our ministries today. Let's look at each more closely.

Power. Like the Pharisees and scribes of Jesus' day, church leaders have established traditions and systems that have become virtually sacred down through the ages. Whether it's declaring that bishops are a special class of believers, that the clergy alone has the right to read the Scriptures, or that one's forgiveness comes from a priest and not from God, the pages of history are filled with examples of power abused in the name of Christ.

Abuses of power in our day are often more subtle. The layout of church office space, the titles we assign, the requirements for membership or for being a teacher—all indicate underlying beliefs about power. Often such things are meeting the deep needs of the leaders rather than serving the people. Like Linus's security blanket in the *Peanuts* cartoon, such externals become a source of great comfort and meet a need for self-esteem and significance, as well. They say, "I'm somebody, and I have the means to prove it."

Because leaders are typically related to institutions, church leadership can become bureaucratic, their chief responsibilities relegated to bringing in money, protecting assets, extending influence, and publicizing programs. But "when church leadership is regarded as bureaucratic management rather than spiritual direction, the credibility of leaders suffers irreparable damage. People resent being manipulated and managed as mere cogs in an organization."[3]

Howard Snyder aptly points out in his book *Signs of the Spirit,*

> Institutions become repositories of vested interests, provid-ing power and security, not easily given up, for those who wield institutional power. . . . Institutions divide people up according to institutional power and status. Generally, institutions make it very clear just where everyone fits— what your place is, and how it compares to those above or below. . . . Institutions define reality in their terms. Right becomes, by definition, what the institution wants, and evil is to oppose the institution.[4]

Such inappropriate vestiges of power must be confronted today as vigorously as Jesus confronted the Pharisees. For power and con-trol are "easy outs," cheap shortcuts that undermine authentic kingdom leadership, corrupting or destroying long-term spiritual fruit.

Paul's criteria for ministry leadership stand in contrast to these symbols of power. In his first letter to Timothy we find a well-known list of qualifications (see 1 Timothy 3:1-13). At the crux of each qualification is a *relationship*—be it family, business, social, or spiritual. Paul told Timothy, in effect: Do not consider an indi-vidual for spiritual leadership until you have examined the integrity of his personal relationships. "Much Christian leadership," Henri Nouwen said, "is exercised by people who do not know how to develop healthy, intimate relationships and have opted for power and control instead."[5]

The question for us, in an age so preoccupied by size, image, and power is: How much significance do we place on the intan-gible qualities that Scripture says are essential for leading by serving?

Authority. All authority comes from God, and He has given all authority to Jesus Christ, His Son (Matthew 28:18-20). Jesus reigns supreme and has authority over the heavens, the earth, and all the authorities and powers of the spiritual realm. Jesus Christ, in turn, has given authority to believers on earth. Howard Snyder has written,

> The church is a theocracy, not a democracy. But it is not hierarchical theocracy tracing from God down a ladder to the lay peasant. Rather it is a family in which God rules supremely, but kindly and lovingly in a way that builds and affirms each member and makes hierarchy superfluous.

Again the emphasis is on relationship, not position. Snyder goes on to say, "The church is not a chain of command but a network of love. This is, of course, supremely impractical to people steeped in hierarchical concepts. But it is the way of the Kingdom."[6] What a world of difference in the relationships and ministry of a group characterized by a network of love rather than a chain of command!

Authority is one component of power. In a sense, power is justified by its perceived authority or its source. The critical issue is whether we are operating from authentic or assumed authority when it comes to spiritual leadership.

> Jesus confronted false spiritual authority in his day: "Then Jesus spoke to the multitudes and to His disciples, saying, 'The scribes and the Pharisees have seated themselves in the chair of Moses.'" (Matthew 23:1) The "chair of Moses" referred to by Jesus . . . speaks of a "seat of authority." . . . Jesus' confrontation is twofold. First, He pointed out that "they seated themselves" in Moses' position—a position given only by God. These men had *taken* authority for themselves, it had not been given to them. Second, the sole basis on which they had grasped this authority was because of their position or rank as Scribes and Pharisees. In other words, their authority was not founded on the fact that they were wise, discerning and true. It was based solely on the fact that they were in charge.[7]

Just as Jesus once overturned the tables of the temple moneychangers, He upended the basis for this kind of spiritual authority. No longer would authority come through a family line or through assumption. Under the New Covenant, the basis for spiritual authority is evidence of the Holy Spirit's work within a humble servant. Moses was the most humble man on the face of the earth, yet he was a powerful man for God's power worked *through* humility.

A leader cannot demand what he has not earned. And earned authority in God's economy is based on humility—a spirit of brokenness before God and man. In his letters to Timothy, Paul did not instruct Timothy to throw his authority into the faces of troublemaking church members. Rather he exhorted: "In speech, conduct, love, faith and purity, show yourself an example of those who believe" (1 Timothy 4:12). Godliness rather than assumed authority was the basis for Timothy's claim to spiritual leadership.

Doesn't all of this simply make sense? After all, one of the functions of the body is to provide us with vision when we ourselves are spiritually blind. Yet leaders who lead by control and power will take one of two directions when their plans are subjected to critique: Some will humbly reflect on the nature and integrity of their practices and repent when necessary, others will make the dissenters the problem and attack them as though they are the enemy.

Sadly, power leaders seldom take the way of humility and repentance. Several years ago I read a letter sent to a local church board. This letter, written by a concerned church member, highlighted some key issues the leadership needed to address. Here are some excerpts (without the real church's name):

Dear Elder,

Thank you for all of the consistent, behind-the-scenes service that you have poured into Grace Fellowship. The fruit of your labors will be seen by heaven and earth one day. Be encouraged!

One promise I made when I accepted membership

almost three years ago was to take problems or concerns
to those who are part of the solution. I would like to take a
few minutes of your time to do just that. . . .

Grace appears to be working from the assumption
that fellowship and discipleship are things that can be
produced through some external button-pushing, transfer-
ring notebooks of information, and skills development.
People don't develop according to set plans and checklists.
To inculcate the fruits of the Spirit takes time. The pro-
gram/pragmatic mind says that you can teach the fruit,
that it will magically appear and you can quantify its presence. How? By having a Fruit of the Month? In four
weeks you'll be kind? In eight you'll be kind *and* patient?
I realize this is a ludicrous illustration, but hopefully you
get my point.

The idea that discipleship can be programmed and
made quantifiable and that its end is just trained bodies
for the purpose of organizational use is categorically
unbiblical. My boss evaluates her business by the bottom
line—numbers, numbers, numbers. She develops me to
make me more efficient and, thereby, more profitable for
the business. With the continual emphasis at Grace on
numbers, numbers, numbers, and the express reason for
all the programs being to get people to serve more efficiently and more profitably—the same underlying principles are tragically the same. We just use more "spiritual"
words for them.

Jesus had an entirely different mindset. He didn't heal
anyone or teach anyone anything because of any other
motivation but love. He valued them. He esteemed them
all . . . and when they were filled with His Holy Spirit, they
responded to this Lover of their souls with obedience,
which resulted in ministry to others. . . .

Do not make "doing it right" your goal, but "to know
Him and the power of His resurrection." The short, the
pragmatic route is not God's way. He is not glorified when
people are burned out, used up, and spending more time

at church than at home with their families. . . .

I look to you as a body of elders to model the life walked by faith and not by sight. Biblical faith asks, "Will it glorify? Will it build up a brother or sister in the kingdom?" Godless, sight-driven pragmatism just wants to know: "Will it work?" . . .

Thank you for your earnest consideration of these concerns. I appreciate the opportunity to share them.

Love in Christ,
Name

The church leadership's response to this letter was insightful. In essence, the board replied, "Your concerns aren't valid because this church has grown by leaps and bounds. People write to us from all over the country wanting to know how we've done it."

The bottom line: Who can argue with success?

This church board based its authority on the cornerstone of pragmatic effort. The church worked well, so how could it be wrong? By all visible standards, by all the eye could see and measure, there was little cause for concern. And since authority was wedded to image and performance, then the basic assumptions—the substance of the issues—didn't require a soul-searching evaluation. *Who can argue with success?* But now, several years later, those early concerns once addressed to the board have proven to be critical issues hindering ministry. Many of the board members have since acknowledged this.

When authority is misplaced in this fashion, a leader implies that others should swear blind loyalty to the institution or move on. And the leader perceives any questioning of the vision or integrity of the ministry as a direct threat.

In contrast, the disciples were sent as ambassadors, fully vested with kingdom authority and backed by the King Himself to be His witnesses to the ends of the earth. The New Testament writers never asserted their own *right* to be heard. Their language was that of emissaries, as bond-servants and apostles who spoke with authority conferred by the only One who held it—the King.

There is a wonderful added benefit to this way of approaching authority: It enables us to maintain relationships that are so crucial to a proper exercise of spiritual leadership. With the position of the King clearly taken, wouldn't hierarchy and titles become so much less important? Here, Jesus alone is receiving all honor, glory, power, and authority. And if we are all equally His servants, then it's easier to view each other as brothers and sisters. We are one people united under the King of kings, people endowed with specific gifts to use in helping one another.

Authenticity of authority is the issue. Does it bear the mark of its originator—the character of the King? Or is one's authority like that of the Sanhedrin, derived from natural, fleshly strategies and structures?

Control. When authentic spiritual authority flows from character, the control exercised by a leader is quite different, both in content and in motivation. Control is always a major concern whenever people consider leadership. We seem convinced that control is essential to good leadership; therefore, leaders should be *in control* of their people. However, the need to control always says more about the leader than about those he or she is trying to influence. "Control freaks" abound in ministry settings.

Control takes many insidious forms. Pressuring people into conformity, shaming their lack of performance, rewarding only what meets our standards, withholding relationship—these are some of the common ways we manipulate with illegitimate control. We move from simply influencing to applying pressure. We reward those who respond, and we neglect those who don't. We give up suggesting, and we start insisting. In so doing, we assume the role of the Holy Spirit in people's lives.

> *Perhaps we haven't yet believed, deep in our hearts, that God loves us no matter what and that He alone is in total control. In our flesh, we constantly attempt to wrest control, even from God, because we fear failure.*

The root of control is our own fear—fear that we will look inadequate or unsuccessful unless others perform as we expect. In its most extreme form, the need for control will insist on defining ministry in terms of loyalty to a particular group and to programs directly attached to the institution. It simply can't allow for freedom and diversity in people or programs.

Doesn't the demand for control simply expose the insufficiency of our basic theology? Perhaps we haven't yet believed, deep in our hearts, that God loves us no matter what and that He alone is in total control. In our flesh, we constantly attempt to wrest control, even from God, because we fear failure.

Yet how little in life are we able to engineer to our complete liking!

Controlling others, even those in our spiritual care, is an unattainable goal. Yes, people may defer to us for a while. But that will quickly come to an end. To think that we can control other people is to believe the lie that got Adam and Eve into so much trouble; they thought they could become like God and be thoroughly independent. Deep down, controllers seem to think, just like Adam and Eve, that being in charge will bring them some prize that has thus far eluded them. But control is only something we grasp at to keep us from facing our dependency upon God and others. Author James Means has written:

> [Often] leaders take action that flows not from a serious, spiritual concern for the welfare of the church and a prayerful discernment of God's will, but from their own authoritarian personalities and desire for control. This kind of behavior often provokes a spirit of rebellion or hostility in the congregation, and it becomes impossible to maintain proper respect and deference.[8]

One manifestation of this type of control is the emphasis on evaluation. Controlling by measuring can provide much comfort and is the essence of pragmatism. An institutional definition of the church requires that leaders devise practical evaluation methods using numbers, forms, appraisals, reviews, state of the church addresses, and committee reports.

On the other hand, viewing God's people as a living body under the headship of Christ requires a more organic kind of evaluation: Is the body being built up? What gifts are being exercised? Where is the body hurting? Are the joints and ligaments holding securely? Are we giving honor to the lesser members?

The apostle Paul performed this kind of spiritual evaluation. In 1 Corinthians 3, he addressed the Corinthian believers as "mere infants in Christ, people who are not ready for solid food." His assessment was of a spiritual nature—not designed to control but to exhort believers to grow in grace. In 2 Corinthians 13:5, he charged the Corinthian believers to examine themselves to see whether they were in the faith. It's true that examination, evaluation, and measurement were a part of the early church, but these things were conducted in a different way.

We would have no trouble in evaluating if we stayed within the limits Paul has already modeled for us. However, we go beyond, trying to measure, evaluate, and control the numbers of converts, baptisms, members, or discipleship groups. Then like King David, we fall into the trap of numbering the soldiers of Israel (see 1 Chronicles 21:1-7). The numbering in itself could hardly be wrong. Rather, it's our dependence on the numbers, our looking to gain our significance from those numbers, that causes us to lose sight of God.

How does it happen? For one thing, the sinfulness of the human heart makes it almost impossible to count without attaching some significance to the numbers. Isn't it interesting that we rarely concern ourselves with measuring the internal values of spiritual maturity, humility, or servanthood? Yet these things are some of the highest values of the kingdom.

Christ evaluated the hidden things of the spirit. His kingdom was made up of the childlike, the sick, the humble, the broken, and those who were demanding miracles in order to believe. With His measure, Christ evaluated the Pharisees and teachers of the Law. He labeled them "hypocrites" numerous times, "blind guides," and "brood of vipers," (Matthew 23:2-33) despite the fact that they had, by pragmatic control, finagled a beautiful temple and attained virtual autonomy amidst the Roman government.

No, Jesus and Paul were not power seekers. They apparently had no need to control, measure, or evaluate ministry in terms of pure pragmatism or organizational success. Jesus made it a point to let the Twelve know that they were not to think in such a way— that's the way the Gentiles thought, and it was shown in the way they lorded it over others. If Jesus considered this mindset to be sinful and counter to the kingdom, then it should also be anathema to us.

I must be very clear at this point. *Not everyone at the forefront of ministry, espousing a vision, is equally suspect.* The body of Christ needs visionaries who serve as catalysts for faith and action. A true visionary, sent and empowered by the Spirit, is a blessing to all. He or she keeps the body sharp, thinking about growth, and pushing the frontiers of evangelism and discipleship.

Sometimes though, a vision is not from the Holy Spirit. What is called "vision" can be merely a "spiritually correct" synonym for personal ambition. Such a vision relies heavily on worldly means and has set its sights on temporal significance. A vision that depends upon the continued presence and positional power of its propagators is not authored by God. Visionaries operating in the flesh promote messages like these:

- "If you're not getting my vision, you're not listening to God, or you are spiritually immature and inferior."
- "This is the only true spiritual vision around here. If you have another vision, we will be unequally yoked."
- "You must remember that you are extensions of the senior pastor [or other position] and are therefore responsible for achieving his vision."
- "You must follow my vision and strategy—it's been proven to work."

Leaders and their followers must constantly discern if the power, authority, and control is coming from a position or from the Holy Spirit working through a humble servant and forgiven sinner. Is the focus always upon the leader and his vision? Or are people consistently directed back to Jesus Christ?

Paul offers the litmus test: "For we do not preach ourselves but Christ Jesus as Lord, and ourselves as your bond-servants for

Jesus' sake" (2 Corinthians 4:5). Any other approach to leadership can lead to serious forms of authoritarian abuse.

■

REFLECT ON YOUR LEADERSHIP

- Think through the ministry organizations and churches of which you have been a part. List those situations in which you've observed power leadership in action.
- What was the outcome of power leadership in each situation listed above? How has this leadership approach affected the leaders? The people?
- Assess the long-term effects of power leadership on the ministry where it is practiced. In what ways is God currently using these leaders and ministries?
- How do you feel about power leaders?

Respond to the challenge

Beware of fixating as the world does on title, image, and being in control.

■ ■ ■

I need Your strength, My Father, to forsake the damaging undergrowth that has confused and obscured my full focus on Jesus.

THE STRUCTURES OF POWER
Abuse Perpetuated Through Systems

WHEN JOHN, A SENIOR PASTOR FOR OVER TWO DECADES, LEFT FOR A new church, Steve, who was much younger and less experienced, was ready to take over.

Steve felt that God had called him to some new ways of doing things in order to expand God's kingdom. While John had done much to help the church grow over the years, the ability to take the church to greater heights in a technologically oriented town seemed to call for a different kind of leadership and decidedly new directions.

As Steve and the new leadership started using innovative, contemporary approaches to spread the gospel, several things happened. As the worship service changed, several people felt their needs were being neglected. The songs were unfamiliar and the sermons were different. Even the pulpit changed! People from the "old guard" felt overlooked and slighted because their traditions began vanishing into air. Some longtime members even spoke of leaving the church.

Steve wondered if he should give in to appease those folks and drop the numerous plans he felt called to implement. As time passed, he began to ask himself, *Am I really God's man to deal with all this?*

OPPORTUNITY AND FEAR

It's a scenario in the world of ministry that repeats itself a thousand times in a thousand ways. A new senior pastor has been chosen. What will happen now to the associate pastors and their responsibilities? Will the new pastor bring in his own team? Whose children will be uprooted and carried to a new location? What about all the marvelous plans people have worked so hard to put in place over the previous years?

I know what it's like in a ministry organization when a few key players are in transition. Everything feels fluid, unsure, tenuous. Everyone wrestles with the same doubts. "Will I have a role—a place—in the new structure? How close will I be to the new leader?"

Change brings a host of fears to the surface. Change also gives birth to a world of opportunity.

As we look at the nature of ministry, I suggest that this sense of opportunity and fear has to do with the concept of structures, or forms. Structure is simply the vehicle for accomplishing ministry in people's lives. It is the program, system, or methodology that carries the life-giving truth of the gospel to individuals in ways that help them believe in God or deepen in their faith.

In the beginning of a new ministry, structure is largely absent. It's a situation that is both freeing and intimidating. New ministries can be wonderful opportunities for fresh creativity and innovation because so few precedents are in place. Who really knows the "right way" to go about the new venture? In this sense, every new ministry feels a little like the new church in Acts 2, where faith, prayer, and dependence on God were the order of the day. That's exciting!

But what actually happens over time, particularly if the new ministry proves "successful"? The structures and forms take on a life of their own. Slowly, they become the focal point—the non-negotiables—rather than the ministry they were designed to serve.

The trend is virtually inexorable because of our human tendency to confuse form and function. Understanding the difference between the two is crucial.

ANALYZING FORM AND FUNCTION

We operate on the principles of form and function all the time. When my legs are tired, I determine that I need to sit down (a function). I look for a chair (a form), and if I find one, I sit there and give my legs a break. But if I'm on a campout or picnic in the woods and there's no chair available, I will look for some other suitable object. I might sit on a huge rock or a fallen tree. The *function* of needing to sit down and rest remains the same; only the *form* (a fallen tree, rock, or chair) changes.

This simple distinction sheds light on what is inviolate in ministry and what is subject to change. Our need to worship, for example, is a basic *function* of spiritual life. It is such an integral part of being a believer that standard *forms* have developed to facilitate it. In the United States, the most common form requires a raised podium where someone stands and leads a group of people arranged in seats facing the front. But this particular form is just one way to arrange for the function of worship.

Another contemporary example of the confusion of form and function is the role of Sunday school in America. Over a hundred years ago, Sunday school was a novel idea designed to reach needy children in city neighborhoods whose parents were unconcerned about the spiritual development of their offspring. No self-respecting parent would think of Sunday school as the answer to her children's needs, which were addressed at home around the kitchen table with an open Bible. Sunday school was for children without a home life!

Sunday school has now become such an established part of the regular church program that suggesting a different approach to reaching children seems like heresy. For many parents, it is the most trusted vehicle for grounding their children in the faith.

Naturally, forms change over time. Women have had to wear head coverings in worship, and the organ was once the only acceptable instrument for music. Consider the changing styles of the music itself: Martin Luther's wonderful hymn, "A Mighty Fortress Is Our God," was once considered too wild and progressive to be sung in church!

Forms of worship vary by culture and country. In Africa, men and women sit on opposite sides of the aisle. In Russian Orthodox services, believers stand for hours during worship services. Certain styles of dress are expected of leaders of worship, too. Some wear robes, others don hats, while still others preach in shirtsleeves.

Unfortunately, preserving the form of worship can quickly become more important than carrying out its true function. The form crystallizes, and any effort to alter it appears to challenge the function. Congregations divide over this! All the while, the crucial element—the function of worship—is overlooked.

Every ministry moves forward on the back of some kind of structure or form. And because it's so easy to confuse form and function, we must become conscious of the structures that carry our ministries, recognizing the direction in which those structures are taking us. It helps to keep two crucial points in mind.

Forms Are Not Neutral
Picture as a triangle the interrelationship between leaders and structures (forms) and the people they lead.

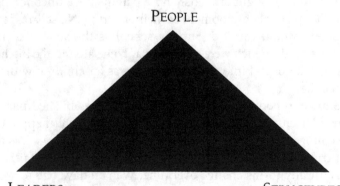

PEOPLE

LEADERS   STRUCTURES

Each of these three entities—leaders, people, and structures—affect one another, and the quality of the interrelationship influences ministry. The structures or forms embedded in our ministries are neither neutral nor amoral. Forms either facilitate or inhibit function; they either foster or hinder real growth and life-change. They can be a blessing or a curse.

A structure can provide a *place* of belonging where people can contribute what God has equipped them to give. It can further the common vision by providing a means for the many to join together toward a mutual goal.

> *The structures or forms embedded in our ministries are neither neutral nor amoral. Forms either facilitate or inhibit function; they either foster or hinder real growth and life-change. They can be a blessing or a curse.*

Ministry forms can also become a curse. Rather than bringing people in and helping them find a place of ministry, structures can create artificial boundaries that proclaim: "You're not one of *us*. You don't do things our way." When forms harden into traditions, they become rote and routine, losing much of their original influence. The words "We've always done it this way" are a death knell to fresh initiative. People with atypical needs or new approaches will ultimately have to look elsewhere.

Forms Are Not Holy

A second thing to keep in mind is that structures have no life of their own. They are only servants of function that either help or hinder real ministry. We must not fall prey to the illusion that rearranging an organization—adding more staff, remodeling buildings, creating more programs—will bring about the desired spiritual results. Structures and forms are not holy in themselves; they can never substitute for the deeper realities of spiritual renewal.

Fallen human nature tends toward reliance upon the forms that support a ministry, rather than reliance upon the Lord. We tend to profane the holy and sanctify the merely temporal and transitory. We come to prefer structure over Spirit.

The Israelites, in the middle of their wilderness journey, grumbled and complained. As a result, God sent poisonous snakes among them. The cure came in the form of a bronze serpent that prefigured the Messiah. Many generations later, in Hezekiah's day, that same bronze serpent was still around. It had become *holy*, an idol to which the people burned incense (see 2 Kings 18:4). This is an example of why true functions in ministry must always be front and center, with forms or structures kept flexible and dynamic. When we invest our trust in structures—in "bronze serpents"—they calcify into obstacles that hinder real ministry. History shows us that great ministries begin with a great vision and great results only to end in power structures and lessened impact.

IDENTIFYING POWER-BASED STRUCTURES

If we were to diagram the inner workings of a power-based structure, it might look like this:

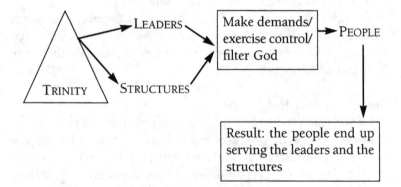

In a power-based structure, the real voice of authority comes from some combination of the leaders and the ministry structures they represent. The focus is on the leaders, who alone are charged with hearing God and discerning direction for the ministry. The leaders filter God's voice and in turn make demands upon the people to fulfill their vision. The people end up serving the leadership and the structure. In a power-based ministry structure, questioning the leadership is a guilt-ridden exercise that comes uncomfortably close to questioning God.

It's important to understand that a power-based structure is like the default setting on a computer. A power structure is the only alternative if we remove Christ as authority in the minds of individual believers and leaders. Without the priesthood of believers, where each person must listen and respond to the Lord, a vacuum develops; it will fill up with the abuse of authority and control. Power-based structures usually emphasize two things:

- *Roles and position.* In power-based ministry structures, you know where you stand in the order of things. The organizational chart may not be visibly printed, but little happens unless sufficient position or power makes it happen. The leader's vision is carried out by everyone "below" him. Decisions, new initiatives, and long-range direction flow down from a select few, with little input from others. An emphasis on role and position, in effect, resorts to ministry by the priesthood of the elite, not by all believers. How different is the New Testament model! There, men and women emerged from Judaism, having lived amidst the Roman military system, with its emphasis on rank and position. Yet those early believers operated as members of the body, in mutual submission to one another and Christ without adapting to their surrounding structures.
- *Control and boundaries.* If leaders subtly present themselves as "the anointed" or as somehow superior in their understanding of God and His Word, and they use that image to demand loyalty, they create an unholy structure for control.

A leader's estimate of humanity is revealed by the way he leads and structures his ministry. If he has a low estimate of humanity, he leads with an iron fist and structures the ministry for tight control. If he views people as sheep, he structures the ministry to gain control of the flock. If church members are merely laypeople, he structures for the clerics to be in charge. If he sees men and women as tools to be used in accomplishing a task or vision, he structures them as employees and puts them to work on the assembly line of ministry production.

If his followers are fellow priests, then he structures in ways that will unleash and free them. If they are brothers and sisters, he works to enhance relationships and to reveal their equality to one other.

RECOGNIZING THAT STRUCTURES CAN SERVE US

Structure and organization are merely tools, or forms, to carry out the functions of equipping the saints and winning the lost world to Christ. Servant-based leadership, as it relates to the people of God and the structures that carry ministry, might look like this:

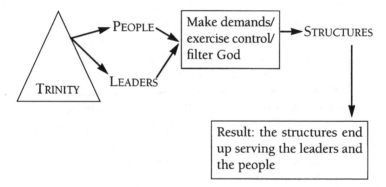

Here the leaders and the people they serve discern the mind and will of God as fellow believers and fellow soldiers in the same cause. In unison, they make demands and exercise control on the structures and organizational systems that exist solely to enable the work of the ministry. The result is that the systems and structures (forms) are constantly changing to meet the immediate needs of the people and the leaders and to accomplish God's work among them.

Our challenge as leaders, then, is to create an environment where the people of God are enabled and encouraged to live out God's purpose in their lives without reverting to the days of the

Judges when "every man did what was right in his own eyes" (Judges 17:6). We must also guard against giving more significance to our ministry forms and structures than they deserve.

In other words, we must not allow our ministry structures to degenerate into forms devoid of their original functions. When that happens, our institutions become entrenched, unchallengeable, and unchangeable.

■

REFLECT ON YOUR LEADERSHIP

- How does the Trinity speak to and/or lead individuals in your ministry? Through leaders? Directly? Draw a diagram (similar to an organizational chart) on the Trinity's influence in the lives of individual believers in your ministry. According to your diagram, in what ways does the Spirit have direct access to each member?
- Is it possible that the Spirit can be quenched through the ministry structure where you serve? If so, what could help solve the problem?
- How does the leadership where you serve influence and/or control the direction of the ministry? In your opinion, where does the structure push the leader into this posture?
- Organizations set boundaries and have membership; therefore, they may also block unity and mutual cooperation with body members outside the organization. Do you agree or disagree with this statement? Why?
- How could organizations more effectively enable the overall unity of the body of Christ to nonbelievers looking on?

Respond to the Challenge

Be aware that power leadership creates or perpetuates the subtle, artificial ways of using or abusing people, rather than serving them.

■ ■ ■

If there is any abuse of people through any leadership forms I am responsible for, Lord, I ask Your forgiveness. Grant me Your releasing power to help transform these structures in order to serve You more effectively.

5
UNDERSTAND THIS CYCLE!
The Key to Renewal

SMELLED THE SMOKE LONG BEFORE I SAW THE FIRE. DARK ONYX clouds, coming from somewhere over the mountains, began to envelop the sapphire Colorado sky. Forty acres of grass, scrub oak, and wildflowers at Glen Eyrie (where I worked) were on fire!

We gathered all available hands to assist the Colorado Springs Fire Department in containing the blaze. Armed with shovels, rakes, water backpacks, and prayer, we battled the hot spots at the rear of the conflagration. The next day, as I surveyed the gnarled, black gash on the side of the mountain, I thought, *I'll be looking at that scar on our beautiful property for years to come.*

AN AMAZING CYCLE AT WORK

To my amazement, God's wonderful creation proved me wrong and taught me a valuable lesson. The following spring burst upon us in brilliant greens, purples, reds, and golds. The most vibrant, verdant growth sprang up where the charcoal and ash had been. In effect, the fall's devastating fire healed the mountain by burning away the undergrowth that prevented fresh, new blossoms.

I witnessed something called *seral succession,* an ecological principle in which, over time, the natural biological systems become so developed that they begin to bog themselves down. In other words, they atrophy. New growth is repressed and beauty lies dormant because the system prohibits it.

Seral succession occurs in spiritual leadership and ministry organizations as well. God sows seeds in the lives of His people, and as these seeds take root, the fruits of His work bloom gloriously. However, as in the natural realm, there is a tendency for such a delicate and intricate arrangement to stagnate. Programs and infrastructures spring up to support and protect a burgeoning ministry. As deadening undergrowth develops, it effectively chokes anything new and different that is attempting to break through. What begins as a dynamic expression of the kingdom of God mires in the trappings of human institutionalism. Slowly, inexorably, the focus shifts to refining policy, drawing membership boundaries, delegating authority, and preserving the status quo. These things replace the earlier dynamism and become the order of the day.

Time and time again, God moves in individuals' lives within the context of their own needs and culture. Then revival and spiritual renewal break out anew, consuming the dead underbrush of institutionalism and frozen faith.

If we observe this type of seral succession down through the ages, we see a spiritual cycle at work in the church. Time and time again, God moves in individuals' lives within the context of their own needs and culture. Then revival and spiritual renewal break out anew, consuming the dead underbrush of institutionalism and frozen faith.

Sinful nature, however, follows the path of least resistance, slowly replacing faith and trust with power and control, preferring to rely on the seen rather than the unseen. Eventually, the grasping chokeweeds of institutionalism and power acquire a stranglehold on the people of God.

Both as leaders and as followers, we have a vested interest in understanding this cycle of atrophy and regeneration. We can get an overview of it by tracing the church's two thousand years of history, briefly exploring the Apostolic Age, the Church Fathers, the 1,200-Year Gridlock, and the Reformation. Admittedly, this will be a whirlwind trip through the vast stretches of sacred history. We cannot do justice to all the details, nuances, and myriad factors that have affected the outcome of the church to this day. For our purposes, however, this survey may at least serve as a brief introduction for anyone interested in further study along these lines. An overview of Jesus' leadership priorities is an appropriate starting point.

JESUS' MINISTRY

Jesus' day was a time of great religious and social ferment in Israel, coupled with a tenuous political stability under the *Pax Romana* (the Peace of Rome). The Jews had settled into life as a conquered people living in an occupied land. With Roman rulers, the Hebrew people weren't truly at home in their own country. The national identity of Israel lay wasted, social mores were in constant flux, and political stability was maintained through detachments of soldiers. The welfare of the common man—let alone that of the infirm, the poor, the emotionally depleted—was of little significance to the leaders of the day. And Roman religion was liberal in the extreme sense of the word. Any set of beliefs and any number of deities was acceptable, in stark contrast to Israel's monotheistic worship of Yahweh.

Revolutionary teachings crashed against the value systems of the day. For the first time since the prophet Malachi, God was speaking directly to Israel through His chosen servant. Jesus brought the Word of God to all people, regardless of their position or condition, and validated their personal worth.

He summed up His mission this way: "The Son of Man did not come to be served, but to serve, and to give His life as a ransom for many" (Matthew 20:28). Jesus' life never contradicted this amazing declaration, unlike the lives of the religious rulers of His day.

While He did meet needs that were immediate and pressing—feeding, healing, teaching, and resurrecting dead relatives—Jesus also met needs that were less temporal. He seemed to focus one eye on the present and another on the eternal. His ultimate priority was the preparation of a people for an eternal household; He was building a holy community.

Christ deemed as most critical, in the entire Torah, two commandments that dealt solely with loving and lasting relationships with God and people. Jesus' concern was for the people of the Law of Moses, not for the rituals or rules. This profoundly threatened the Sanhedrin, the religious elite. And Jesus completed the offense by publicly exposing the bankruptcy of the legalism that had come to define Judaism, condemning the leaders who imposed it on the people.[1]

In all His preparation of the twelve disciples, Jesus never emphasized any continuing organization. Nor did the heart of His teaching convey any single verbal formula. When He was betrayed, Jesus prayed that His disciples might be one and that all those who were to believe in Him through their word might be one. While this certainly implied a close and continuing fellowship, it hardly specified any visible structure.[2]

At the time of His ascension, Jesus instructed the disciples to wait before they went anywhere or did anything; God alone knew what should be done and how. Their part was to adopt an attitude of readiness and obedience. He said their roles were to be His witnesses. He then left His disciples gaping at the heavens, armed with the knowledge of His identity and the memory of His ministry. His death and resurrection must have loomed big in their minds as they struggled with kingdom principles that didn't make sense until the Holy Spirit arrived. Finally they understood: He had left them with the daunting task of invading the world with the good news.

SUMMARY OF JESUS' LEADERSHIP PRACTICES

- Jesus publicly confronted the power-oriented, legalistic system and its leaders.
- His leadership style was that of a servant, even though He truly had all the power and authority of heaven.
- He instructed His followers in unity, love, and servanthood, teaching the importance of community.
- He did not speak of an organization, institution, or any specific structure through which the apostles were to facilitate the spread of the gospel.
- When the religious establishment sought His death, He submitted.

THE APOSTOLIC AGE

Jesus' ministry didn't just disappear with Him into heaven; His physical life here on earth was only the beginning. He informed the Twelve that upon His departure the Holy Spirit would come to continue His ministry.

> And He, when He comes, will convict the world concerning sin, and righteousness, and judgment . . . [and] He will guide you into all the truth. (John 16:8,13)

In other words, the Holy Spirit in the lives of believers — enabling them by the same power that raised Jesus from the dead — would fulfill the Great Commission. Thus Jesus looked for those who would persevere in the face of inevitable opposition, people through whom He would accomplish His work. As Jim Petersen wrote in *Church Without Walls,*

> Jesus never said or did anything to indicate that structure and organization could serve to protect God's people. Shepherds and servants, yes, they would be needed, but He never talked about structure. Not that He was against structure. It is necessary . . . but for protecting His people He had something far more trustworthy — the Holy Spirit.[3]

The apostles believed Christ's words. They entrusted themselves, the work of the kingdom, and their fellow believers to the Holy Spirit. Frankly, they had nothing else to rely upon. There was no shelter to be found within religion. The Jews viewed the Christian gatherings as a heretical sect, and they habitually harassed, arrested, and sometimes murdered its leaders.

The one thing Christians did have in common with their Jewish counterparts was their adamant refusal to participate in the idolatry of the Romans.

Neither were the Jews a social force. Those drawn to follow Jesus in the early years typically came from the middle and lower classes.

The sense of separateness and of community was so strong that the Romans considered the believers in Christ to be somewhat clannish. Politically, the Romans operated on two clear premises: Religion was the cement of the empire, and a common religion guaranteed civil peace. This insistence on a polytheistic base opened the way for the waves of persecution that washed over the community of believers (and Judaism) for the next three centuries.

With temporal opposition firmly entrenched, the early followers longed for the return of Jesus and the coming of His kingdom. Peter, John, Paul, and the other leaders of the day exhorted the followers of the Way to be "alert and sober" (1 Thessalonians 5:6, 1 Peter 1:13). The belief that Jesus could appear at any moment had a purifying effect on the community, for "we shall be like Him, because we shall see Him just as He is" (1 John 3:2).

The priority of the apostolic church was the same as Christ's — to build a holy community.

> You are no longer strangers and aliens [to one another], but you are fellow-citizens . . . you also are . . . being built together into a dwelling of God in the Spirit. (Ephesians 2:19,22)

With this in mind, early church members minimized hierarchy and permitted the Head of the body to direct its ministry and missionary efforts. The Holy Spirit played a living role in the lives of the brethren. Women had a place in ministry, exercising all of the various gifts of the Spirit, as did men. Most significantly, every believer recognized his or her responsibility for growing the body and spreading the gospel.

False leaders, with doctrines committed to undermining this approach, appeared in the community, espousing everything from adherence to Jewish rituals to reliance upon secret Gnostic knowledge for salvation. Yet there was a conspicuous absence of power leadership or organizational tactics in combatting these false leaders and movements.

The apostles instead brought the gospel and the supremacy of Christ to bear on these issues. Christ's death on our behalf, His resurrection, and the lifelong impact of the gospel on the individual and community—these had to be the focal point, they seemed to say. Christ is our all in all. He has all authority in heaven and on earth. If we abide in Him we will bear fruit.

Surely Paul and the apostles strongly considered the use of tight organizational control and the use of power and authority to produce the desired results. They had seen these things in action around them. Whatever their considerations, they chose to emulate Jesus' example of serving and teaching.

They served the saints by confronting the false doctrines and leaders with Truth. The truth and relevance of the gospel for all of life, they believed, was sufficient. Real power lay in the nature of God, who took on human form, died, and rose again. The saints responded because the Spirit indwelt them and guided them into truth.

The leadership styles of the apostles reflected the humility and service of their Lord. Peter referred to himself as a common "fellow-elder" (1 Peter 5:1). He never took the title or claimed the position of Chief Apostle (or, in our modern day lingo, CEO).

John, the hotheaded young disciple who wanted to call down fire upon faithless Samaria (Luke 9:54) referred to Gentile believers as "little children" and "beloved." John ultimately proclaimed that love for one another was the litmus test of knowing God. "The one who does not love his brother whom he has seen, cannot love God whom he has not seen. . . . The one who loves God should love his brother also" (1 John 4:20-21).

Peter, Paul, John, James, and the rest were steeped in Judaism, while many of the unnamed local leaders were probably converts from Roman paganism. The temptation to structure according to the familiar—filling old wineskins with new wine—was tremendous, particularly when problems ran rampant. Yet, they continuously entrusted themselves and those under their care to the Holy Spirit.

Before Paul set sail for Jerusalem, he gathered together the Ephesian elders (where the Holy Spirit, not tradition or ambition, had made them leaders) and exhorted the believers to be on guard against false teachers. Paul did not instruct them to "strategize this way" or "organize that way" as a defense. He did not instruct them to name a CEO or senior pastor. Neither did he draw up a clear organizational chart to send to the entire Ephesian church. Paul could have easily done these things. After all, the Roman culture had very clear lines of authority, and all of its subjects knew the chain of command.

Nevertheless, Paul echoed Jesus' statement that the Spirit was the only One capable of protecting and advancing the work of the kingdom: "I commend you to God and to the word of His grace, which is able to build you up and to give you the inheritance. . . ." (Acts 20:32).

THE CHURCH FATHERS: A.D. 100–325

The early church had a lot going for it. Increasing numbers of people were following the teachings of Jesus. A huge informal network of itinerant apostles, prophets, teachers, and evangelists went from place to place, equipping the saints toward the goals of love, unity, and fullness in Christ. It was attractive, to say the least.

As the body grew, after the death of the first-generation believers and apostles, the human propensity to walk by sight reared its ugly head. People are more comfortable seeing a representative of God than being directly in communion with the Living One. Second- and third-century believers saw that theirs was a unique religion, but it was still a religion. Thus they began to set up structures and leadership not unlike the well-known Jewish and pagan infrastructures. They

SUMMARY OF THE APOSTLES' LEADERSHIP PRACTICES

- The Trinity was the real and practical leader of the early church.
- The apostles gave themselves to building up God's people rather than to organizations or hierarchies of leadership.
- Women exercised their spiritual gifts in ministry.
- The leadership style of the apostles flowed from a desire to serve rather than dominate. Their demeanor exuded humility, not pride or arrogance.
- They did not set up organizational structures to combat ever-present doctrinal or leadership problems.
- They taught that the indwelling Holy Spirit's ministry of leading and truth-giving would overcome the attacks from within and without.

soon forgot that Jesus was the head of the body as they began to transfer His leadership to human leaders and the supporting administrative structures.

Not long after John died, seral succession began in earnest. To be sure, the Romans were growing more antagonistic toward anyone who disrupted the empire by refusing to participate in the state religion. The Roman leaders were convinced that the reason the empire's luster was starting to fade was that their gods were angry at the loss of allegiance in favor of the Christian God.

Persecuted from the outside, and torn by divisions and heresies from the inside, the second generation of church leaders certainly faced daunting decisions. In reality, the pressures they faced weren't so different from those the apostles had weathered. However, instead of entrusting themselves to the Holy Spirit and developing a community based upon His fruits—love, grace, forgiveness, perseverance, and wisdom—they resorted to more pragmatic approaches.

Their solution? Create a tighter organization. First, to refute certain false teachers who claimed lineage back to a specific apostle, the leaders produced a similar line of succession all the way back to their own apostle. Second, they determined that basic rules of order needed to be written down for general distribution to the fellowships. Thus, *The Didache* or *Teaching of the Apostles* was compiled. This was essentially a manual of discipline, giving guidelines for life and worship.

Third, and most significantly, the foundational model of leadership changed. Ignatius articulated a doctrine significantly different from the servant model of Jesus and the apostles.

> This church leader from Antioch "wrote a series of letters. In these, he speaks habitually of a single bishop in each church, a body of presbyters and a company of deacons. God's grace and the Spirit's power, he [taught], flow to the flock through this united ministry."[4]

Ignatius advanced the idea that leaders were a special class of believers by declaring "the bishop is representative of God the Father and the presbyters are the sanhedrin of God. . . . Nothing was done without the bishop. . . . [Ignatius stated] that he who honors the bishop shall be honored by God."[5] This was a radical departure and without precedent. In the apostolic age, individuals who sought out such distinctions and power were rebuked. For example, the apostle John marked Diotrophes as a man who loved to be first and sternly rebuked him (3 John 9). Yet, as the doctrinal heresies increased and became more insidious, leaders convened further to systematize beliefs and organizational structures.

> Their motives were to "Unite all believers in conscious fellowship; spread the gospel in its purity; bring all believers into a visible "body of Christ." In practice, the three [motives] proved to be . . . contradictory, for in the process of defining the faith and of developing an organization, bitternesses arose which were a palpable contradiction of the love which is the chief evidence of Christian unity."[6]

The leaders separated the church into competing organizations, each having its own hierarchy, and excluded those who would not submit to the leaders and institutions. Whether consciously or unconsciously, they began to lead and structure according to the same pattern of the pagan religions that surrounded them. A special class of priests held power over the spiritual well-being of those under their charge. The worship became increasingly formulaic, with decreasing participation by believers. Leaders adopted a distinctive style of dress and claimed special rights— the ability to grant forgiveness, to withhold the Lord's Supper, and to teach the Scriptures. As the clergy class became more defined, the casual observer may well, at times, have mistaken the church for just another mystery cult.

Undoubtedly the church fathers had noble intentions. They wanted to prevent the spread of heresy and bring some sense of unity to a far-flung group of adherents. But at what price had they achieved their goals? A kind of clergy/laity caste system usurped the ministry of "average believers." And this system is still in place today.

THE 1,200-YEAR GRIDLOCK: A.D. 325–1517

The church fathers unwittingly created a system ripe for abuse. Each prerequisite law and prefabricated litany locked the gospel behind another set of doors and placed the keys in the hands of a few men.

SUMMARY OF THE CHURCH FATHERS' LEADERSHIP PRACTICES

- They transferred leadership from Christ—the Head—to human leaders and administrative structures.
- They set up structures and infrastructures similar to Jewish and pagan religions.
- Ignatius taught that the bishop represented God. He thus set up a hierarchy of bishops and priests.
- Early leaders separated the church into competing organizations.

In the early years of the third century, Christianity gained not only the protection of the state but also the endorsement of Emperor Constantine. Like his predecessors, Constantine instinctively knew that a social fabric reinforced by a religion could keep his tenuous political power alive throughout the diverse realm. Due to his recent conversion, rather than reverting to the old Roman deities (which were now out of fashion anyway), he designated Christianity as the new state religion.

Enjoying new legitimacy, church leaders began to mirror levels of the political hierarchy in order to administrate the new, uniform church. Constantine proclaimed himself *Pontifex Maximus*—where the state and church joined. Pagans became "converts" for political purposes, and sound theology took a secondary place to keeping control of the masses. The distinction between the called-out ones of God and the world became blurred.

Augustine supported this trend, calling for an even closer alliance between the state and the church. He felt that the state needed the church to transform society and that the church needed the state to enforce that transformation. In order to achieve uniformity among the people, political force and power came into play. Sadly, the persecuted became the persecutors. One writer called this "a fearsome arrangement."[7]

Spiritual power progressively moved into the hands of a few men. The bishop of Rome assumed a greater role among the churches, ultimately assuming the title of Pope. Gradually, the hierarchy of the monarchical bishoprics centralized in Rome. The common people found themselves at the mercy of either the spirituality or the corruption of the clerics.

The final transfer of power into the hand of a single individual came during the papacy of Gregory VII. He declared that the pope could use any available means to substantiate his authority, *even if it contravened Scripture.* As the earthly guardian of Scripture, this was within his right.

Rampant abuse of power and all its trappings by the Roman church, combined with the hopeless passivity of the people, led to a church millennium with little evidence of the gospel's reality. The Holy Spirit broke through repeatedly, though, raising up individuals with burning convictions. These faithful disciples proclaimed that the Imperial Church asserted power the gospel had never granted.

Columba, John Wycliff, Peter Waldo, Geert Groote, John Hus, and others kindled sparks that burned away some of the undergrowth that had choked the life of the church. They propagated such radical ideas as moral reform within the clergy and the proclamation of Christ—rather than Peter—as Head of the church. They asserted that the laity could confess their sins to one another and had the right to read the Bible for themselves. For this and for preaching the gospel to the masses, many of these individuals were persecuted and sometimes murdered.

Just as the Pharisees and Sadducees feared losing power and control over people, the institutional church sought vigorously to protect its political position and its perceived status as intermediary between God and people. If either of these eroded, those in power would lose their position, livelihood, and security.

What began as a shift in assumptions by Ignatius in the second century evolved into a full-fledged spiritual system. One man was designated as the physical head of the body on earth. Jesus became more and more a mere figurehead for His Bride.

However, the sparks of renewal and reformation refused to die out. In this era, they culminated in the flame of the Reformation. It blazed across Europe, led by a Spirit-filled monk named Martin Luther.

THE REFORMATION

On October 31, 1517, the die was cast for the Reformation. Infuriated by indulgence-peddling clerics, Martin Luther nailed his theological platform to the door of Castle Church in Wittenburg. His ninety-five theses called the church to move beyond calcified institutional structures to the pages of Scripture as the final authority for faith and ministry.

SUMMARY OF THE 1,200-YEAR GRIDLOCK EVENTS AND TRENDS

- Roman Emperor Constantine designated Christianity as the state religion and himself as Pontifex Maximus, joining Rome and the church.
- Augustine supported the state/church marriage and called for even closer ties.
- Gradually a hierarchy of bishops centralized in Rome.
- The Holy Spirit repeatedly broke through this atrophy, bringing the gospel once again to the common person.
- Repeatedly, renewal movements were attacked by threatened institutional leaders.

During this period, Luther, John Calvin, and others sought to refocus on faith in Christ as the sole means of salvation, to restore purity and integrity in leadership, and to reinstate the priesthood of all believers in practice. They made great strides in these areas, particularly in publishing the Bible in common languages.

The second wave of reformation in the sixteenth and seventeenth centuries brought along a group known as the Anabaptists. To them, the Reformation efforts had not gone far enough. The Anabaptists pushed the starting point of right thinking about God's design for the church back to its New Testament roots.

However, once power was wrested from the Roman Church, new structures and new hierarchies began to grow in their place. Within a relatively short period of time, reformation groups became state churches in their own right. Then they were as quick to defend their power and structures as was the Roman Church before them. Lutherans and Calvinists dealt with the Anabaptist movement by arresting its leaders and sometimes murdering them.

For all the good that came out of the Reformation, it still serves to illustrate our stubborn tendency to use human means of power to build a manageable, controlled system. To have repudiated the papal system was remarkable. But the Reformation did, indeed, fall short. It failed, in many instances, to return to the Scriptures and to the Spirit that empowered its movement toward Christian liberty. How tragic!

In the last four hundred years, many groups have built upon the work of the Reformers. Moravians, Methodists, the modern missionary movement pioneered by William Carey, and various church and parachurch movements in the present have all sought to return to the Scriptures as the sufficient rule for faith and practice.

Eventually, seral succession strikes movements, churches, and organizations. They turn to the secular community for their structures and motivational principles and begin building a leadership model based upon secular values, assumptions, and principles. Like Israel of the Old Testament, they begin to tolerate, accept, and even proliferate the culturally accepted "high places" where idolatry thrives.

SUMMARY OF THE REFORMATION LEADERSHIP PATTERNS

- Catalytic regeneration began with the Reformation, when the Bible and salvation by faith were restored to the common people.
- Eventually, the Luther- and Calvin-led reformation movements retrenched and formed their own version of state churches.
- A second-wave Reformation, led by the Anabaptists, met stiff resistance from the first-wave reformers.
- The cycle of atrophy and regeneration has repeated itself frequently since the Reformation era.

ARE WE LEARNING FROM HISTORY?

Someone once said that what we learn from history is that we don't learn anything from history. But by looking back, around, and inside ourselves, we may indeed discover what hinders and what facilitates the work of God in a particular day and time.

As we look back over church history we see that in the beginning of any true spiritual movement, the Holy Spirit is released as men and women exercise faith and courage. God honors the simple, stumbling efforts of His children as they step out in faith. As people move into uncharted territory toward a vision He's given them, God meets them there.

Yet, when their efforts meet with a measure of success and renewal breaks out, an insidious, counteractive process begins. The underbrush of institutionalism begins to take root. The human tendency is to build an organization around this living, dynamic thing called ministry. Then the surrounding structure becomes a heavy, cumbersome weight that cuts off the spiritual light and nutrients necessary for growth. In this process of institutionalization, people come to rely on human figures at the helm. God's Spirit is quenched; freedom and innovation decline.

As leaders grow more entrenched, they invest more power and authority in their position. The priesthood of the elite increases and the priesthood of believers declines. An invisible caste system develops, making a subtle distinction between laity and clergy. Laity learn to step back out of the picture, find a comfortable place to sit, and watch the "professionals" at work.

As any ministry takes on an organizational focus, something to protect arises. Assets, property, history, and tradition must be preserved. Eventually the light and life that produced them lie dormant, and it seems that tradition and structure are all that remain. Thus, as institutionalism takes over, reformers of almost any kind meet with resistance and suspicion. They appear to be challenging the unchallengeable.

> From the institutional perspective, any kind of renewal movement immediately provokes suspicion, if not actual hostility. A new structure dedicated to church renewal is intuitively, and correctly, perceived by the keepers of the institution as calling into question . . . the validity of the institutional church itself . . . in its given form.[8]

Wouldn't it be helpful for church leaders to understand this human digression from spiritual renewal to spiritual stagnation? Surely it is crucial to resist the human tendency to resort to strategies of power and control to bring about spiritual results.

Suppose we see our role as servant charged with the responsibility and privilege of helping others come into the fruitful expression of God's vision for their part in the kingdom. Then we may avoid the temptation to build our own kingdoms to which we recruit others with their time and talents.

Of course, if we continue to focus people's eyes on Christ, we will not be the "Maypole" around which everything revolves. And that may be painful. Yet, in this way, the ministry itself will not calcify into an organizational structure that requires loyalty and protection as it moves further from the Holy Spirit's leading.

■

REFLECT ON YOUR LEADERSHIP

- Reflect on the beginnings of your church or ministry. If you were not around then, ask some of the pioneers about the early years. Or read materials that record the history. What vision for ministry did the founders begin with and pursue?
- In your opinion, is seral succession affecting your church or organization? In what ways?
- Is seral succession affecting its leadership roles? Your role? How?
- To what extent do your ministry responsibilities require you to protect the institution? What are the costs to you, personally? To others?

Respond to the Challenge

Cultivate continual repentance and spiritual renewal in your personal life, avoiding the path that leads toward "power leadership."

■ ■ ■

*Lord, give me grace to lead others as You have led me,
with a gentle voice and gracious goodwill.*

6

THEOLOGICAL FOUNDATIONS
The Precedents for Spiritual Leadership

THE NIGHT WAS GROWING OLD, AND THE ELDERS MEETING SHOULD have ended thirty minutes earlier. Instead, the discussion was just beginning to pick up steam. On this particular evening, some heavy-duty questions about church leadership had bubbled to the surface.

Before the group got any further, however, one man glanced at his watch and said, "Folks, this is really important stuff, but it's almost eleven. I move we keep this discussion going at our next meeting."

A number of heads nodded. But just as someone started to second the motion, another elder stopped everyone short with his comment. "I'm not so sure about that," he said. "Around here, we do what works. We've always done what works. The style of leadership we've been using has gotten us where we are as a church. I think we're wasting our time talking about something as intangible as *leadership*."

A small chorus joined in, both pro and con. Finally, on a purely practical basis, they tabled the discussion, thinking: *Someday, when we've got the time, maybe we'll look into the subject in depth. Right now, other things are more pressing—like membership, maintenance, programs, budgets, personnel. . . .*

SPIRITUAL LEADERSHIP: A SECONDARY CONCERN?

I wish this particular elders meeting was the only occasion in which ministry leaders have avoided the fundamental questions of spiritual leadership. However, the topic often receives secondary attention, for at least two reasons. First, perhaps we're not convinced that spiritual leadership is all that different from leadership in other human affairs. The popular assumption today is that the methods and values of the business world are right and good because, for the most part, they seem to work. Pragmatism is the guiding light.

If we're looking for a written-on-tablets model of leadership, then we will be disappointed. . . . While God has not given us a formula or rigid prescription, neither has He left us groping in the dark, waiting on the next new management seminar to give us direction.

Second, we may wonder if the Bible has anything definitive to say on the subject of leadership. It's not like the issues of saving the lost, caring for the poor, or praying for guidance. The very word—leadership—has a secular ring to it. And we might remind ourselves: Christ never laid out a clear blueprint for how to lead.

If we're looking for a written-on-tablets model of leadership, then we will be disappointed.

But if we look to the triune God, we see that He has modeled leadership for us. His leadership values and principles are everywhere in the Scriptures. While God has not given us a formula or rigid prescription, neither has He left us groping in the dark, waiting on the next new management seminar to give us direction.

As we've seen, leadership in the body of Christ means more than just taking business practices and overlaying them with a few Bible verses. Spiritual leadership operates on a different frequency. Its validity and worth cannot be weighed by human scales because the source of power lies outside the individual leader; both the means and the end are subject to the control and direction of Another.

By saying, "We do what *works*," we declare that the Bible has little to say about how we as leaders operate. If measurable results are the focus of a ministry, then we adopt anything that heightens the results or appears useful. It's called following the path of least resistance.

The Scriptures offer an alternative. The Bible comes replete with themes that offer both boundaries and insights into godly leadership. These guidelines function like the left and right field lines on a baseball diamond. They show us what's fair playing territory for the context of spiritual leadership. They also tell us when the ball goes foul.

With regard to spiritual leadership, the playing field (or context) looks something like this:

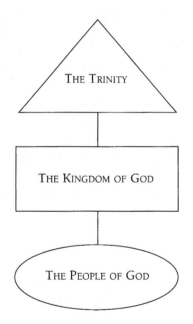

As we endeavor to define the boundaries for spiritual leadership, we can focus on three familiar biblical subjects: the Trinity, the kingdom, and the body of Christ. These grand and glorious themes speak to God's design for spiritual leadership in fresh and freeing ways.

THE TRINITY

The progressive testimony of God from the pages of His Word tell us that He is one God and that He exists as three co-equal persons.

- Hear, O Israel! The LORD is our God, the LORD is one! (Deuteronomy 6:4)
- God is spirit; and those who worship Him must worship in spirit and in truth. (John 4:24)
- "Go therefore and make disciples of all the nations, baptizing them in the name of the Father and the Son and the Holy Spirit." (Matthew 28:19)

Relationship is at the core of the Godhead, and in that relationship we see the fundamental spiritual principles regarding leadership.

At every stage of redemption we see how the Father and the Son and the Holy Spirit relate to each other. "In the beginning God created the heavens and the earth. . . . And the Spirit of God was moving over the surface of the waters" (Genesis 1:1-2). Paul wrote of the part the Son plays, "In Him all things were created, both in the heavens and on earth, visible and invisible" (Colossians 1:16).

Even before creation, the Trinity together planned the redemption of mankind. The Father purposed the "Lamb slain from the foundation of the world." The Son would enter the creation to become the Lamb Incarnate and shed His blood on our behalf. The Holy Spirit would act as Comforter and Teacher, indwelling those who embrace the Lamb by faith and continuing to reveal the Christ.

What we see in the Godhead is an incredible picture of interdependence, and of unity and diversity, where the One *leading* and the One being *led* change according to need and contribution. Equality is the basis of their relationship, yet there is also role differentiation among the Trinity. They share authority, yet each has a different function. There is no jealousy or competition in their midst — only harmony and unity. Theologian J. I. Packer put it like this:

Within the complex unity of His being, three personal centers of rational awareness eternally co-inhere, interpenetrate, relate in mutual love, and cooperate in all divine actions. God is not only *He* but also *They*—Father, Son, and Spirit, co-equal and co-eternal in power and glory though functioning in a set pattern whereby the Son obeys the Father and the Spirit subserves both. All statements about God in general or about the Father, the Son, or the Holy Spirit in particular, should be "cashed" in the Trinitarian terms, if something of their meaning is not to be lost.[1]

As we delve into the topic of spiritual leadership, what is the relevance of this interaction of the Trinity?

THE IMPORTANCE OF THE TRINITY FOR LEADERS

We can glean significant messages that are applicable to leaders by observing the operation, interrelationship, and outworkings of the Godhead.

- Among leaders, there ought to be unity yet diversity.
- At the human level, there should be multiple, not singular, leadership among God's people.
- Leadership is neither hierarchical nor organizational; it is relational.
- Power struggles, jealousy, and competition have no place; they destroy relationship.
- Relationship, not the task of the organization, should be the glue that holds human leaders together.
- The final goal should be to direct people to the Trinity, not to the leader or the organization.
- The possibility of "shared authority" flows from the model of the Trinity.
- Though we are all brothers and sisters before Him, we have unique roles and contributions to make.
- Respect for one another and dependence upon God are the qualities that mark our character as spiritual leaders.

- Leaders must be listeners and learners. If the Holy Spirit indwells all, then we need to listen to Him *through others*. This means repenting of any pride that puts us in opposition to God or produces a sense of superiority toward others.

If the example of the Trinity were better reflected in our practices of spiritual leadership, we would see a blessed difference in the way we operate with each other. Greater unity of heart would prevail, and leadership would manifest itself in others-oriented acts of service. Our prevailing leadership style would be based on the model of servanthood, with the final focus resting on the example of our triune God.

This is pretty heavy theology, and you may be wondering how it applies to day-to-day ministry operations. Let me share with you how this worked out in "real life" within our CoMission ministry. In 1992, I was given the responsibility of forming—developing the processes and structures—and overseeing and leading the functions of CoMission Training and Materials. CoMission's goal was to send large numbers of mostly American laypeople to the former Soviet Union. The strategy was to help public school teachers learn how to use a Bible-based morality and ethics curriculum in their classrooms. CoMission's partners included over eighty-four denominations and ministry organizations, so this was a big task—bigger than anything I had ever dreamed possible.

The total effort during five years of ministry would include seventy training events for fifteen hundred laypeople going to eight countries in the former Soviet Union and distributing 6.5 million pieces of literature, Bibles, and videos. The budget for these aspects of the work would exceed ten million dollars. The rest of CoMission generated costs far greater. This magnitude of work was on my shoulders from day one.

It doesn't take a rocket scientist to see that this type of thing can't be done by one person alone. The Lord brought the right people along to partner with me and share the load of leadership.

They all are people who exercise servant leadership and thrive when they work together. Let me introduce some of them to you.

- Ralph, my longtime friend, can see the big picture—the complexities of various organizational and people issues—as he designs curriculum and other training systems. He quickly analyzes and understands cultures and is the author of one of our premier training tools, *An Introduction to the Russian Soul.*
- Andy has an amazing ability to bring levelheaded leadership to complex organizational and people issues. He understands the fine points and big issues of corporate finances and projects where the group is going. With great wisdom he can help steer the group in effective directions. He is highly respected by all who know him and watch him lead.
- Eddie is the most cross-cultural guy I know. He is Creole by birth, yet is quite able to minister fruitfully among African Americans, Hispanics, Russians, and Anglos. He speaks and can minister in three languages, and has his morning devotions in the Greek New Testament on top of that. He is by far the most versatile person on our team and has served in more roles and worn more hats than any of the rest of us.
- Myles was one of the pioneers in Walk Thru the Bible and helped in the development of Walk Thru's early training materials. Myles has the unique ability to frame ideas in clear form. He is the shepherd among us, while also functioning as a dignitary/ambassador. He has enormous respect and credibility among the leadership of CoMission. He is our best training designer.
- Dennis hears what is being said in vision and theory and helps bring it into reality with concrete plans and processes. He tries to bring order out of chaos, so things go smoothly and efficiently. He has a spiritual way of dealing with issues and is always bringing individuals to prayer about their circumstances. Dennis makes things

happen, and he does it in a spiritual way, all the while seeking to maximize the potential of others.

- Christine has an enormous capacity for getting things done and running training events. She is as comfortable doing this in the former Soviet Union (where administrative tasks are much more time consuming) as she is in America. She makes great observations about what is happening in the bigger picture and helps execute solutions. Christine has the respect of all of us who watch her as we wonder how she pulled off still another training event. Until she joined us, we were all dying under the administrative load of running our training conferences.

- John loves to study the Scriptures and teach. He spends hours in Bible study every week and regularly sheds tears over what he sees. When John teaches, people immediately sense his love for the Bible. John has been an extremely versatile member of our team and has developed quite a gift for fund-raising—a needed talent in our ministry.

I could talk more about Lois, Bill, Cheryl, Curt, Paul, Bob, Bette, Rex, Andria, Jeri, Eva, Jenifer, David, Darrell, Lynn, Dick, and many more. But I'm sure you get the picture.

The point is, I am the one charged by my organization to be responsible for all of this. If something goes wrong, we all need to look carefully at what happened and what God is trying to teach us. If something goes right it's because we followed the Spirit by using principles that have their roots in the example and model of the role differentiation, the relationships, and the functional leadership of the Trinity.

For example, we work as a team, depending on one another's strengths and roles. We recognize and deeply respect each other's callings, strengths, spiritual gifts, and contributions. We have roles to play because of our gifts, and we each offer leadership to the group in those special areas. Our focus is to recognize what God wants to accomplish, to look to the best person to bring leadership to it, and then to support him or her in that process. We practice mutual submission and are quick to defer to one another. This is what we term *rotating functional leadership*. Each person has a function, and when that function is needed, that person becomes our leader.

In Ephesians 1 the Father adopts us as sons (verses 3-6), the Son mediates our salvation (verses 7-12), and the Spirit seals our inheritance (verse 13). Each plays a part, and each has a role. This is functional leadership in the kingdom.

THE KINGDOM OF GOD

I was talking with a friend in another city recently. I asked him, "How's the church going these days?" I expected him to catch me up on some of the happenings in his congregation, but his response stopped me short. "Well," he replied, "we have a new pastor fresh out of seminary, and we're off and running down the same old road every other high-powered young seminary graduate travels to make his kingdom look like it's God's."

His words startled me and set me wondering. *How much of my life as a ministry leader would be leveled under that indictment? How much of my effort has been about proving myself as a leader at the expense of others?*

Clearly, the question "Whose kingdom am I building?" is a central one. Sometimes in our enthusiasm we run down those tracks of personal kingdom building. Unless we cling to the kingdom of God and its values, we'll quickly fall into the trap of trying to build our own kingdom while calling it God's.

The kingdom has been misunderstood throughout the ages, despite being one of the focal points of Jesus' teaching ministry. How can we define it? The definition I offer of the kingdom of God is this: It is God's sovereign rule for all eternity over creation, the spiritual world, nations, kings, and individuals.

When we say the words in the Lord's Prayer, "Thy kingdom come," we are in essence praying that our lives will be involved with giving others the chance to put themselves under the rule, rather than the wrath and judgment, of the King.

Jesus told the disciples at His ascension that they were to go and do kingdom work and that His kingdom would grow. The kingdom of God was an integral part of the teaching and ministry of the early apostles as they went from place to place, starting ministries and shepherding existing ministries. Acts 1 begins with the disciples' question, When will the kingdom come? (Acts 1:6). The very last verse of the Book of Acts describes Paul: "Boldly and without hindrance he preached the kingdom of God and taught about the Lord Jesus Christ" (Acts 28:31, NIV). The kingdom is so central a focus that Paul declared that all of history will culminate with one act—when Christ "delivers up the kingdom to the God and Father, when He has abolished all rule and all authority and power" (1 Corinthians 15:24).

The Scriptures tell us that Citizenship in this kingdom comes through faith in God's provision for our sins. His grace bestows forgiveness as a gift.

Whoever comes to God by faith is a citizen of the kingdom, a member of His universal and invisible church. Being a faithful member of His kingdom is our goal and highest calling.

These are simple, fundamental truths that we can easily overlook. When our focus shifts away from these truths, we begin to build our kingdom rather than God's kingdom.

THE IMPORTANCE OF THE KINGDOM FOR LEADERS

- The King has absolute authority. All citizens of His kingdom are equal under His reign.
- A church or organization is not synonymous with the kingdom of God.
- Building our own personal kingdom means hindering the progress of God's kingdom.
- Building ministries that focus on human leaders is contrary to kingdom values.
- Effective kingdom leadership is measured by character and relationship. It is empowered by the Holy Spirit, not one's position or personality.
- Organizational structures should help extend kingdom citizenship to others while demonstrating kingdom values.
- Spiritual leaders are to point people to God's kingdom, not their own kingdom.

THE PEOPLE OF GOD

The Bible could be called "the book of relationships." From cover to cover we find God's people in relationship to and with Him, with each other, and with the world of people around them. From eternity past God determined to fill His kingdom with people who are purchased by the blood of His Son—all for the purpose of eternal fellowship.

In order to appreciate the significance of being part of the people of God, or being a leader among the people of God, we need to remember what happened at Pentecost. In Old Testament times God's Spirit "came upon" particular individuals at specific times. In that day a leader such as Moses or Joshua was the direct link between God and the people (see diagram below).

The situation changed after Christ went to be with the Father. From that point on, the Holy Spirit made His home in the life of each and every believer. God's people, then, are actually made up of individuals who have the very life of God moving in and through them. Leaders no longer have a monopoly on being led by God; all believers have access to His leadership.

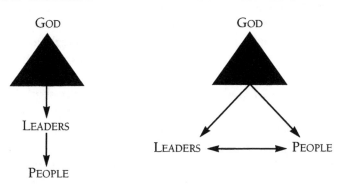

OLD TESTAMENT

GOD

LEADERS

PEOPLE

NEW TESTAMENT

GOD

LEADERS ⟷ PEOPLE

The truth that the church is the people of God is so wondrous that it can't be contained in one or two New Testament descriptions. Indeed, a number of metaphors describe what it means to be God's people: the Bride of Christ, a royal priesthood, a purchased possession, the body of Christ, a spiritual building. But the most familiar term for defining the people of God is "the church."

With every generation since the time of Constantine, however, the word *church* has become more and more synonymous with an institution, a building, or an address in a particular locality. Lost to us is that true biblical sense of being a part of the church—God's people unleashed to do His bidding.

Neither is the church made up of nonprofit organizations with corporate names that include "church" or "fellowship" in their titles. The church is all the believers in a local area. Dr. Joe Aldrich, former president of Multnomah Bible College, said, "There is one church in Portland, Oregon. Until the church rediscovers this truth there will be no power."[2] With this in mind, some pastors and leaders have financed a new sign on the main roads leading to their city that says, "The Church of Salem, Oregon, welcomes you. We meet at the following locations." As leaders, part of our calling is to restore people to that larger sense of being part of what God is doing in our day, not just in our particular little church or organization but through His church worldwide.

Paul most often relied upon the phrase "the body of Christ" to convey the meaning of being God's people. A person has only one head. Jesus is the Head of His body, and He alone is able to supply what the body needs to function. He gives direction; He maintains contact with every part; He gives us a role to perform for His own purposes. And He declares each of us, from the seemingly least to the greatest, equally necessary and significant.

The people of God, in an intimate new relationship of being members of one another, are marked by several key traits. These form some of the parameters that should guide our relationships in the body. As a body we are called to function in love, in service, in mutual giftedness, and by "one anothering"—as brothers and sisters in community. Let's look at these qualities a little closer.

Love

Our relationships are to be grounded in love—in an expression of self-giving—that furthers the growth of another. We are not bound to each other out of duty or ulterior motive, using those around us to further our cause or accomplish a task. Toward the end of his life, John—as the only surviving apostle—could have pulled rank on everyone in the body. Instead he wrote and spoke about love and its preeminent importance among God's people and their leaders.

Serving

Seven different Greek words describe serving in the New Testament, with over 250 references. As a whole, this indicates the major emphasis the early church placed upon serving one another in the church and in the world. Serving others is to be an integral expression of living and functioning together in the body of Christ.

Mutual Giftedness

Each of us has been given spiritual gifts, which means we all have a part to play and a contribution to make to the whole. Spiritual leaders who want to serve Christ's people need to help others identify and maximize the gifts God has given them. There are no insignificant contributions.

"One Anothering"

Almost seventy times in the New Testament we are admonished to "one another" each other. We are to make a range of contributions in each other's lives that is vast and far-reaching. We are told to encourage one another, bear each other's burdens, build up, admonish, teach, and rebuke one another. Our relationships with one another are to be a significant part of the transforming power of the gospel in our lives.

Brothers and Sisters

Throughout the Bible, believers are called brothers and sisters. We are members of the same spiritual family, with God as our Father. No matter what roles we perform in the church, we stand shoulder to shoulder, beset by the same struggles and sharing the same joys as brothers and sisters in Christ.

Community

As members of the body of Christ we are meant to live in community with one another. Community isn't based on physical proximity; it describes the interworking of our lives together. We rejoice in and accept the fact that we need each other. We are friends and part of the spiritual family of God. Community is the mysterious dynamic of believers that makes the whole greater than the sum of its parts.

Christ said that our relationships with each other are so significant and so central to the gospel that He gave the world the right to judge the validity of His message by the love they observed among us: "By this all men will know that you are My disciples, if you have love for one another" (John 13:35).

As He prayed on the night before He died, Christ asked the Father to make us one so that the world would know the Father loves us with the very love that flows among the members of the Trinity: "I in them, and Thou in Me, that they may be perfected in unity, that the world may know that Thou didst send Me, and didst love them, even as Thou didst love Me" (John 17:23). Our role as leaders is to strengthen and encourage relationships among the people of God so that our unity is indeed a visible witness to the reality of Christ.

Clearly, leadership in the spiritual realm does not follow the same principles and practices as the world around us. We have been given a different blueprint. Spiritual leadership is to be profoundly determined by the ways in which the Father, the Son, and the Holy Spirit relate as members of the Trinity. The vision is greater, the focal point being Christ and His kingdom. The nature and character of spiritual leadership reflects the humble stewardship of those Christ has called as members of His body, the people of God.

Toward the end of His life, Peter addressed leaders with carefully chosen words. A crown of glory awaited them if they had faithfully shepherded God's flock without thought of personal gain, position, or power (see 1 Peter 5:2-4). Perhaps Peter was particularly aware of the temptation to build one's own kingdom while calling it God's. It is the most sordid of human motivations—to claim the glory for ourselves—and the one easiest to disguise in spiritual garb. In the end, it will leave us as empty and alone as those we had hoped to serve.

■

REFLECT ON YOUR LEADERSHIP

- This chapter lists three overarching biblical themes—the Trinity, the kingdom, and the body of Christ—that provide the boundaries for what spiritual leaders are to be and to do among God's people. What other overarching themes might have a similar influence?
- Evaluate your ministry practices. Better yet, ask a sampling of people to evaluate your ministry practices by answering the question: How am I doing at living out the implications of leadership—using the Trinity as a model—within the kingdom of God and with the people of God?
- Each section in this chapter lists some major implications for servant leadership. What other implications could you add, based upon your own experience or observation?

Respond to the Challenge

Look to the biblical themes of the Trinity, kingdom, and people of God to give boundaries and focus to your leadership practices.

■ ■ ■

Lord, I humbly submit to Your full reign and ask for Your strength to follow the model of the Godhead. Build Your kingdom and not mine. Help me always to relate to Your people in love, just as You do with me.

7

SUPERSTARS OR SAINTS?

The Average Believer in Ministry

A S I LOOK BACK ON MY LIFE, I'M THANKFUL I DIDN'T REALIZE WHAT was supposedly required of a person to be a leader in ministry circles. I came to Christ in the army during the Vietnam War. Within a few months I began to tell others in simple, at times cryptic, ways the difference Christ had made in my life. Before long a small group of individuals were willing to study the Bible with me—people who overlooked the obvious fact that I was still charting these spiritual waters myself. They probably didn't give much thought to whether or not I was qualified to lead them. They simply followed.

WHO QUALIFIES?

I look back on my first fumbling attempts at discipling with a grin and a thankful heart. Though my efforts were awkward and unpolished, God honored them. And I remained blissfully ignorant of my thoroughly unconventional approach to spiritual leadership.

Yet I know the church insists upon designating a special category for leaders, and I would never have qualified for the distinction. The approach is that of an armed services recruiter—"The Marines are looking for a few good men"—a mindset that largely ignores the counsel of Scripture. We tend to think of leadership qualities in this way, as though God were the chief recruiting officer inspecting the troops, singling out the few who qualify for an elite spiritual leadership corps. Those who don't measure up to this standard can return home to pursue their own interests and ideals.

> *The real ministry, whether large or small, is often reserved for the trained professional, and "ordinary" folks cower in the background, quietly convinced that "average" is a dirty word. In the process, the body of Christ atrophies.*

Those who do qualify for this "spiritual aristocracy" have degrees and diplomas, titles and position. Whatever the job—counselor, Sunday school teacher, ministry director—the applicant need not apply unless he or she is highly trained or gifted in public ministry. The real ministry, whether large or small, is often reserved for the trained professional, and "ordinary" folks cower in the background, quietly convinced that "average" is a dirty word. In the process, the body of Christ atrophies. A host of needs goes unmet and multitudes of believers mistakenly assume there is no place for them to serve.

Much of this mindset originates from a faulty concept of what a spiritual leader is in the body of Christ. We're often directed to Old Testament examples as justification for the "leader-as-superstar" model. Moses, the great deliverer, single-handedly led a downtrodden people out of bondage. Joshua was the consummate military leader. Nehemiah motivated thousands to undertake a huge building program. And David, who made it to king, held great civil and spiritual authority. In Israel's theocratic age, these men spoke for God. The followers followed, as was appropriate for the time.

Note, however, that the first-century disciples did not return to the examples of great Old Testament leaders. When searching for the ways and means to lead this new movement of the Spirit forward, they didn't look backwards to Judaism or to the patriarchs for their leadership model. Instead, *Christ was their model.* They were citizens of a new kingdom. Leadership there would be different.

We need to immerse ourselves in the fact that God used ordinary men and women to accomplish His work. Peter and John were rough fishermen, not professors. Matthew, the tax-gatherer, would have come in last in anyone's popularity contest. Lydia spent her days selling elegant fabric in the marketplace. None was a leader in his or her own sphere.

The significant players in the New Testament church were not superstars. Rather, they were average men and women who had courage and simple faith, men and women gifted by the Holy Spirit to play their particular parts in a drama that Someone else had written. They were nonexperts whom God used in powerful ways. And He used them despite their lack of religious credentials. He used them because of their faith in Him. If we can view early believers and leaders as the ordinary men and women they were, our concept of who and what a spiritual leader is will be radically altered.

In the last part of the twentieth century, the church groans under the weight of a flawed assumption that its spiritual leaders must be well educated, professional, and high-powered in order to be considered legitimate and worthy. The church as a whole pays a steep price for this false distinction, and these requirements create a dangerous pedestal from which leaders can fall.

Of course, it wasn't that way in New Testament times.

LEADERSHIP IN THE NEW TESTAMENT

The disciples recognized something fundamentally different about the way the church of God was meant to operate after Christ gained access for us to the heart and throne of God. There was no going back to old models and methods.

Three differences in particular should influence our perceptions about spiritual leadership. Each of these differences has a bearing on the role a leader assumes and where he or she fits into the overall picture. Leadership patterned after New Testament models does not rely on one central authority figure (as in the days of Moses and David) because Christ provided for us a new basis for relationships, a new source of power, and a new means of growth.

A New Basis for Relationships

Christ's disciples didn't see themselves as "junior Nehemiahs" charged with the task of discerning God's mind for His people and then instructing everyone accordingly. Jesus instituted a different order based on the mutuality and interdependence typified in the "one another" commands. We are to love one another, serve one another, put one another first, comfort one another—the list goes on and on. In fact, we are supposed to do so many things for each other that it takes sixty-nine verses in the New Testament to fully describe "one anothering." Jesus' model of leadership in His body emerges from a relational context in which life, power, and leadership come from our relationships together in the Lord.

Jesus inaugurated a new basis for leadership among His people. He said, "You are not to be called 'Rabbi,' for you have only one Master and you are all brothers" (Matthew 23:8, NIV). And again, "I no longer call you servants, because a servant does not know his master's business. Instead, I have called you friends, for everything that I learned from my Father I have made known to you" (John 15:15, NIV). Relationships in His kingdom do not exist on a hierarchical basis, with someone being over one person and under another one. Rather, we stand and fall together, shoulder to shoulder, brothers and sisters in a common spiritual family.

Christ transcended the human barriers that would normally divide and separate us as individuals—race, gender, and background. In Him, "there is no distinction between Greek and Jew, circumcised and uncircumcised, barbarian, Scythian, slave and freeman, but Christ is all, and in all" (Colossians 3:11).

Relationships are the basic building block of His kingdom. *At its core, spiritual leadership must be relational in nature.* To violate the basic relational nature of the body is to transgress the bounds of spiritual leadership. When we violate this irreducible minimum, we reveal that our leadership concept comes not from the Spirit but from the world around us. Unfortunately, most churches and organizations view leaders as employees. It's no surprise, then, that their leaders treat other members of the body as lower-level employees rather than fellow laborers. The leadership model we choose will directly determine whether or not we experience relational fallout in the body as a whole.

The Relational Nature of Spiritual Leadership

Note: The numbers in parentheses refer to the references recorded in the NIV.

A New Source of Power

Spiritual leadership is also affected by another fundamental difference between the Old Testament and the New. Before Christ, God's people relied on a human figure to spiritually instruct and guide them. But Christ said that when He went to be with the Father, someone greater would come to instruct and guide us. Now the Holy Spirit takes up residence in our hearts to teach and lead us. We are no longer left solely dependent on human leadership because the Spirit Himself guides, convicts, and instructs us according to the will of God (see John 14:16-17,26; 16:7-15).

When Jesus said, "I must go away but I will send the Holy Spirit in My place," a natural response is to feel that we got the short end of the deal. Once again, God became hidden. But the reality of the Holy Spirit means that we carry His power *within us*, rather than experiencing Him outside of us, as the disciples did. Because He lives in us, we can do and be and speak what we would not normally be able to.

This new source of power enables every follower of Jesus to influence others spiritually — to be a leader in some manner and realm. Leaders no longer have to be viewed as the ones who make it all happen. This eliminates an elite model of leadership, which can be so discouraging to the untrained follower of Jesus.

Great comfort and peace flow from knowing that the Holy Spirit enables all believers to fulfill God's unique purpose for them. Leaders cooperate with that process of spiritual enabling, but they do not have to carry the weight of it. The advent of the Holy Spirit made the Old Testament model of leadership obsolete and a superstar mentality, at best, unnecessary.

A New Means of Growth
Every believer makes a gifted contribution to the growth and health of the body of Christ and to the furthering of His kingdom. This is done through the various gifts of the Spirit given for the common good (see 1 Corinthians 12:7). In this sense, each believer can be a leader in the arena of his or her particular gifting. Conversely, every believer and leader is a follower as well. This happens when believers defer to one another in the areas of their gifts.

A number of gifts are commonly thought of as "leadership gifts." Ephesians 4:11 speaks of the gifts of apostle, prophet, evangelist, shepherd, and teacher. Romans 12:8 also lists the gift of ruler or of leadership. Be aware that each of these gifts actually links to a unique way of leading. An apostle will lead by laying the foundation of a ministry or overseeing ministries that cover large and diverse groups; someone gifted in teaching will lead by communicating spiritual truth in such a way that others learn and develop. So, while every believer is a leader in his or her area of gifting, God still gives individuals particular gifts for the general oversight of the body of Christ. The chart below offers an overview of the New Testament leadership gifts.

Gift	Primary Passages	Clear Example	Functions / Characteristics
Apostle	1Corinthians 12:28 Ephesians 4:11 Many others: We know more about the gifts of the Apostles than all the other gifts combined.	The Eleven Apollos Barnabas James Paul Timothy Titus Others	1. Innovating and pioneering new ministries 2. Correcting existing ministries 3. Completing what is lacking in existing ministries 4. Usually mobile in their ministries 5. Trans-local ministry oversight and influence
Prophet	Romans 12:6 1Corinthians 12:28 Ephesians 4:11	Agabus Phillip's daughters Barnabas Judas Silas	1. Sees issues and implications clearly and speaks to them forcefully 2. Corrective of existing ministries 3. Often predicts upcoming events
Evangelist	Ephesians 4:11	Phillip Paul	1. Constantly reaching out to the lost 2. Sees issues related to reaching the lost
Shepherd	Ephesians 4:11		1. Constantly ministering to/guiding the saved 2. Sees issues primarily related to building up the saved
Teacher	Romans 12:7 1 Corinthians 12:28 Ephesians 4:11	Paul	1. Constantly studying the Scriptures 2. Focused primarily on understanding and propagating right living based on the Bible
Leader/ Ruler	Romans 12:8	James	1. Tends to see a direction to take in the midst of complex issues 2. Constantly serving a group of believers

Leadership's Bottom-Line Values

The wise use of spiritual gifts is the cornerstone of the kind of "every man" ministry we see in the New Testament church. The leadership of believers is the oil by which the church is meant to run. Every person has a unique part to play. The role of those who lead is to help others find their particular contributions. Leaders "have as their mission not 'to minister' but to prepare God's people for *their* ministry!"[1]

While certain gifts provide the body with leadership, there is no justification in the New Testament for a special category that places "leaders" in a separate position above all others. We have a great High Priest who mediates between us and the Father. He has made each of us members of His royal priesthood. In the final analysis, *we are all leaders who lead by serving the Lord and each other through the Spirit's work and unique gifting in our lives.* According to Dr. David McKenna, "every Christian is called to be a follower of Christ and a leader of others."[2]

Isn't it comforting to realize that spiritual leadership is not governed by a one-size-fits-all mentality? There's room for variation and diversity according to our calling and gifting. However, consider these bottom line core values that inform the best kind of spiritual leadership.

A Growing Intimacy

It almost goes without saying that in order to lead or influence others spiritually, a person has to be deepening his or her own relationship with the Lord. We can't offer to others Living Water that we haven't yet tasted (or fail to drink from regularly). Christ likened us to branches that grow and flourish as they are attached to the Vine, which is Christ Himself. He tells us that no matter how gifted or talented we are or how much we know, if we do not abide in Him our efforts will be wasted (John 15:1-6).

A growing intimacy with Jesus stems from the everpresent New Testament triad of faith, hope, and love. These streams of spirituality are meant to converge in our lives, to carry us forward toward maturity. We can't be deficient in one of the three for long without that lack of sustenance somehow robbing us of the benefit of the other two. A lack of hope, for instance, will make faith quite difficult and make love seem meaningless.

Spiritual leadership, in contrast to secular leadership, depends directly on the internal realities of the one who is leading. We influence others for Christ as we grow in our own faith, hope, and love. Our influence grows out of the fertile soil of personal spirituality. It stems not from *what* we know but from *Who* we know—and how well.

Character

Another irreducible minimum for spiritual leadership is character. We may be able to compensate for lack of experience, skills, or education—in many areas of leadership. But deficiencies in character will contradict our message and undermine our credibility. People receive the things of the kingdom not only by what they hear; they must see it and experience it as well. And they experience it in their leaders (1 Corinthians 4:17).

Perhaps this is why the majority of Paul's requirements for elders and deacons in his letter to Timothy have to do with personal integrity and character. He says that elders and deacons must be "above reproach, the husband of one wife, temperate, prudent, respectable, hospitable, . . . gentle, uncontentious, free from the love of money" (1 Timothy 3:2-3). All of these words express important character qualities.

Authenticity

Webster's gives a definition of authenticity worthy of significant consideration. It says succinctly that authenticity means "being actually and precisely what is claimed." Further, Webster's says that when someone or something is authentic, it is *authoritative* because it conforms to an original, reproducing essential features.

The basis of true power in church leadership is the power of personal spiritual authenticity. Spiritual authenticity is the validity of the Word of God and the Spirit of God demonstrated in the lives of leaders. People who lack such authenticity should not be entrusted with authority or official positions in the church.[3]

An insightful individual once noted that character is "who you are when no one is looking." If my character is authentic, then it will be consistent with what I profess, even when no one is around. It will be as evident when I'm leading a Bible study or board meeting as when I'm driving in traffic, talking with my kids, or walking the dog. If I claim to be a spiritual leader, indwelt by the Holy Spirit and being conformed to the image of Christ, then my life should increasingly display His character qualities. This authenticity becomes extremely attractive as the beauty of Christ shines forth in my life.

Integrity

Integrity is the integration of lifestyle and belief so that they become one. Proverbs 11:3, NIV, says, "The integrity of the upright guides them, but the unfaithful are destroyed by their duplicity." Proverbs 10:9, NIV, says, "The man of integrity walks securely, but he who takes crooked paths will be found out."

> Unless leaders are perceived to be people of outstanding integrity they cannot lead for long. If they lack integrity, leaders will be revealed eventually for what they really are: manipulators, power grabbers, or exploiters. They will be rejected by followers.[4]

First Timothy 3 and Titus 1 also discuss the issue of elder qualifications. Consistency of character and the presence of integrity are the measure of true leadership. It is important to look at the *whole* life, not just the ministry life, according to Paul. Look at each person in the different roles he or she occupies: employer or employee, neighbor, husband, father, member of the community. Is he living as a disciple of Christ—established, rooted, and growing in grace—in all these settings? Does his life bear the marks of true character, which are integrity and authenticity?

Humility

Consider for a moment a verse in Hebrews that is often quoted with regard to spiritual leadership: "Obey your leaders, and submit to them; for they keep watch over your souls, as those who will give an account. Let them do this with joy and not with grief, for this would be unprofitable for you" (13:17, NIV).

The Greek word for *submit* here is *hupeiko,* and this is its only appearance in the New Testament. The word could be translated here as "yield," "give way," or "be persuaded by." In the context of Hebrews, the latter fits best because leaders who spoke the Word of God urged the Hebrews to imitate their faith and, therefore, to be persuaded by their speaking and by their lives. Submission here conveys the idea of allowing oneself to be influenced deeply by the words and life of a leader whose character is consistent and evident. It is not a situation of blind kowtowing to a leader's authority.

How would the combination of "leading" and *hupeiko* actually look in a church? I have watched a church closely over the last several years. The pastor of this new, rapidly growing church has had to deal with the care and oversight of a significant influx of people. He spent a long time researching the various ways other churches handled this desirable problem and found perhaps five or six ways he could approach it. People responded to his leadership in this, not because of his thoroughness of research, but because he has a gentle, humble way of leading. *They saw his character and were persuaded by his spirituality.* They submitted to his leadership because of his godly example, not because of his Senior Pastor title.

In other words, a sterling character, a growing intimacy, authenticity, integrity, and humility—these are the qualifications of leadership. And they are fruits budding from a long incubation period, rooted in the hidden places, manifesting themselves first in small things. Can you imagine a weekend leadership conference with smallness and hiddenness as the primary topics? These are not subjects for which we usually hunger, yet they are crucial to spiritual leadership.

The ministry of small things is among the most important

ministries we are given. . . . Small things are the genuinely big things in the kingdom of God. It is here we truly face the issues of obedience and discipleship. It is not hard to be a model disciple amid camera lights and press releases. But in the small corners of life, in those areas of service that will never be newsworthy or gain us any recognition, we must hammer out the meaning of obedience.[5]

A leader is not to be evaluated by his position, achievements, theological training, or natural abilities. What he knows or has learned must have had time to germinate and manifest itself in the warp and woof of his life. Traits like self-control, humility, and faithfulness become the barometer of one's fitness to lead.

> *The question is not, "Does the leader have followers?" but rather, "Does the Lord have followers as a result of the leader's influence?"*

What true spiritual leaders reflect to those around them, however imperfectly, is the character of Christ as they know Him internally. The author of Hebrews said that Jesus was "the radiance of [God's] glory and the exact representation of His nature" (Hebrews 1:3). Jesus' claims and the way He lived were in agreement. This is an apt description of the character of a spiritual leader: His word and his life match up.

The heart of spiritual leadership, then, is serving people—looking out for what is best for them rather than using them as the means to a larger end. The question is not, "Does the leader have followers?" but rather, "Does the Lord have followers as a result of the leader's influence?"

Paul encouraged Timothy to aspire to the role of being a leader in the body of Christ, but not because leadership represented being a cut above everyone else. Rather, Timothy was to view his leadership position as a place from which he could offer to others what God had conveyed to him.

Spiritual leadership does not belong in the exclusive domain of the superstar. We limit the Holy Spirit when we make leadership an exclusive fraternity of those with up-front, public gifts and dominant personalities. In other words, spiritual leaders contribute from their individual giftedness. Their role is to help keep the body of Christ healthy and functioning well. This kind of leadership cannot be limited to a few; it requires something from each of us.

◼

REFLECT ON YOUR LEADERSHIP

- The chart on page 105 places spiritual leadership in the context of relationships in the body of Christ. We could say "Whatever spiritual leadership is, it cannot violate these relational boundaries and still be God-honoring." Do you agree? Why?
- How does one become a leader in your ministry? What are the criteria? What differences do you see between the criteria you listed and those indicated in this chapter?
- How would you describe the "relational climate" among people in your ministry? What are some of the contributing factors related to leadership practices?
- How are the people in your ministry viewed: as employees, laypeople, or something else? Explain.
- Call to mind a leader who took the role of a "junior Nehemiah" with his ministry. What were the organizational results of this approach? What were the consequences for the people? For other leaders?

Respond to the Challenge

Recognize God's right to design and utilize "average" believers to accomplish His purposes. Then attempt to maximize those you serve, humbly accepting your own limitations.

◼ ◼ ◼

Help me, dear God, to have a greater impact for You by doing what is best for Your entire body.

AWAKENING THE SLEEPING GIANT
The Believer's Unique Arena of Service

SEVERAL YEARS AGO, CHEST PAINS AND A BAD CASE OF BURNOUT GAVE me pause to consider the question of spiritual gifts with more than intellectual curiosity and forced me to see the significance and wisdom of what the Bible teaches about an individual's role in the body of Christ.

I had laid aside my role as a leadership developer and innovator of new ministries in exchange for a position managing a major conference facility with twenty-three buildings (including a small castle). There were a hundred employees to look after as well. While this was a far cry from my normal contribution, I clung to all the usual good reasons that prompt anyone to accept such a responsibility: The need was immediate and pressing, and I was the most logical person to call on.

Every day as I got dressed to head off to my new job, I kept telling myself that if I tried hard and trusted God enough, I could rise to the occasion; God would honor my faith. And every day the tasks of replacing asbestos in the basement or tackling new marketing strategies left me depleted. The function I served was important to the kingdom, but I was not drawn to it nor was I gifted for it. I slowly began to recognize my chest pains and lack of motivation for what they were trying to tell me: *I really wasn't designed for this!* I had sincerely responded to a pressing need. But now I felt physically tired, emotionally drained, and chained to a prison cell.

Where had I gone wrong?

DRAGGING THOSE CHAINS

Being the wrong person in the wrong ministry for the wrong reasons, and performing the wrong functions, had its *right* side! The truth that "God has placed the members, each one of them, in the body just as He desired" became an ironclad reality to me.

I know that if anything is normative in the body it is diversity. We each have different gifts and differing motivations, and we are drawn to various ministry needs accordingly. This diversity of gifts and contributions is a clear New Testament teaching. Yet for eighteen hundred years the church has minimized it. Why? What steered us off course?

During the second century, in an effort to ensure doctrinal purity within a growing and far-flung church, a manual on church discipline was published in Syria. It was called the *Didache*. This document curtailed the use of the spiritual gifts and removed responsibility for spiritual leadership from the laity to a new class— the clergy, the ministry professionals. The individual believer was shackled and restrained from realizing his or her unique contributions to the body through the gifts of the Spirit. The *Didache* may have been effective in thwarting a few pockets of heresy, but it served to clamp the church in chains. We still drag those chains today. Long accustomed to letting a few professionals take care of the "real" ministry, millions of laypeople remain passive, rarely forging beyond the official or unofficial limits relegated to them.

A relatively recent secular and economic phenomenon has reinforced this bondage. The Industrial Revolution brought us its mass production quotas and standardization mentality. The underlying assumption in industry was, "We can put out more products faster if we streamline the production and standardize the product." As this kind of philosophy invaded the church, it produced something akin to a "McChristian." Individual distinctiveness and contributions were blurred, usually in favor of doing more faster.

The tendency toward producing McChristians flows from two questionable assumptions. First is the premise that *believers can be mass produced.* The idea is that by repeating the same steps, in the same order, with steady attention, one can produce maturing believers in a manner similar to mass-produced burgers and fries. During the process of assembly, the McChristian focuses on the picture of the perfect believer. He or she takes in a set of standards for spirituality, and any deviation from this norm will indicate a spiritual problem or unfaithfulness.

> *The Industrial Revolution brought us its mass production quotas and standardization mentality. . . . As this kind of philosophy invaded the church, it produced something akin to a "McChristian." . . . The idea is that by repeating the same steps, in the same order, with steady attention, one can produce maturing believers in a manner similar to mass-produced burgers and fries.*

McChristians are made to be interchangeable, as well. If one person in the assembly line falls away, anyone can take her place. The only two requirements of operating in the assembly line are a volunteer spirit and a belief that God will see him or her through.

The second questionable assumption is that *believers are omnicompetent.* The theory is that a committed follower ought to be able to do it all. Mrs. Jones, if she really tries, can teach, lead, serve, and counsel—or whatever else needs to be done—with results that would parallel those of any other equally committed believer. If a person is sufficiently motivated or adequately taught, somehow he or she can pull it off. But is this realistic?

The average person feels this heavy weight of excessive expectation. If he's not careful, his life will become a revolving door of Bible studies, personal evangelism programs, committee meetings, seminars, and financial pleas. He must have a regular quiet time, pray for many hours, get involved in missions, be a great parent, disciple new believers, and more. The weight of these "ought-to's" becomes almost more than he can bear. Many people have tried with good hearts and sincere intentions to comply, without success. Some have even left the church, feeling inadequate and thoroughly unspiritual.

These underlying messages — that believers can be mass-produced and are omnicompetent — breed a value system that produces great guilt. Few can measure up to the demands pouring forth from the standardized ideals in our mass-production oriented society. Guilt becomes the pervasive feeling of "average" believers in our day. Those who excel at the accepted standards usually turn professional. They enter full-time ministry; they become heroes. "Just look at everything we're doing," they seem to say. "If you try hard, you can do it too. *If you have enough faith.* . . . "

FINALLY: WAKING UP!

If we compare the body of Christ — God's people through the ages — to a sleeping giant, then we'll be encouraged to see the signs of its awakening. A growing number of believers are earnestly seeking their unique niche of service in the body of Christ. This is one of the healthiest trends for God's people in this century. So much latent power and potential exists in an energized laity whose members are freed to contribute their unique talents.

When we, as servant leaders, begin to help individuals discover their gifts and callings, we must start with them where the Bible begins with each of us: at the place of worship and surrender. Paul reminds us in Romans 12, before he launches into the topic of spiritual gifts, that any real service grows out of worship. "I urge you . . . to present your bodies a living and holy sacrifice . . . which is your spiritual service of worship" (Romans 12:1). Ministry is not a task, program, or production. It is an act of worship by people who acknowledge that God's great mercy has redeemed them for the purpose of relationship with Him, for sacrifice, and for service to others.

Paul's next words are crucial to our understanding of the task of enabling people to find their niche of service. "For through the grace given to me I say to every man among you not to think more highly of himself than he ought to think; but to think so as to have sound judgment, as God has allotted to each a measure of faith" (12:3). In warning us against the temptation to see ourselves as omnicompetent, Paul advises us to avoid living beyond our limits. We should think of ourselves with sober judgment in accordance with the measure of our faith. This implies that each believer, and each leader, has clear limits set for him or her—limits of capacity and gifting.

"For . . . we have many members in one body and all the members do not have the same function," Paul continues in verse 4. There is no standardized believer, no phantom ideal, no "McChristian" in Christ. If we spend our energy chasing after that mirage, we may never discover our own purpose and calling. We will miss out on the blessing of making our unique contribution to the body and to the Great Commission.

Imagine a beautiful painting, an intricate, involved rendering of life. Imagine the rich variety of colors brushed on the canvas—the blue hues of the sky, shades of green in the grass and trees, yellow and orange of sunlight, black to add depth and shadow. What a dull picture it would be if each element were painted the same color, or only a few shades were represented. In the same way, God intended the whole spectrum of color and diversity to be represented in His children. Some of us are to be blue, yet each with a unique hue; others are designed to be tones of green or brown—like the earth—while others are yellow like the sun or a daisy. Each color provides depth, beauty, and variety in God's painting of His family.

As leaders in the body, we must be even quicker to acknowledge the essential diversity of its members. Diversity, not standardization, is the norm. *It is important that we not impose our own gifts and limitations on those we lead.* Our job is to further the process of helping individuals discover their contribution and learn to live within their God-imposed limits. With this in mind, let's look more closely at the two interrelated principles of *spiritual gifts* and *spheres of ministry*.

Pursuing That "Born For" Feeling

God has given to each believer one or more spiritual gifts. As recipients, we do not have a say in the particular gift we receive, for "he [God] gives them to each one, just as he determines" (1 Corinthians 12:11, NIV). Further, we are to view our gifting as our primary personal means of ministry to others (1 Peter 4:10).

Paul refers to an individual's spiritual gift as a "manifestation of the Spirit" (1 Corinthians 12:7). It is astounding to realize that the Holy Spirit chooses to reveal Himself to the world through the outworking of spiritual gifts within the body of Christ. When gifts are permitted to operate freely with their supernatural diversity, a fuller manifestation of the Spirit is revealed in the body and among the lost. Conversely, when manmade shackles of conformity and standardization chain this diversity, the work of the Spirit is quenched, opening the door to all manner of spiritual ills.

Spiritual gifts facilitate the ability of the body to derive its growth from Christ. Colin Kruse wrote, "As the 'gifted' believers function properly, the church grows as a body, drawing its power for growth from Christ the head."[1]

Once, while I was attending a conference for ministry leaders, a friend admitted to me the disappointments surfacing in his life. "I now realize that I came into the ministry out of peer pressure," he said. "I kept trying to build this large and glowing ministry, but it just never happened." He told me how he was beginning to think about his contribution differently and was beginning to understand his spiritual gifts and limits. The years of frustration and discouragement had not been the result of insufficient faith or some hidden sin.

"Finally, last year at age forty," he said, "I began to conclude that what I was facing was a gifts-and-sphere issue. Now I'm asking a different set of questions. *What has God designed me to do? What are my gifts and sphere of ministry?*"

He realized that God had historically used him not in a large ministry but in small-group and individual ministries. He had the ability to work in-depth with people. Breadth, organization, and preaching would never be his specialty. Instead, he began to move into a pastoral counseling role and experienced greater satisfaction—and spiritual fruit.

God gifts us not for our own good but for the good of the whole. In using our gifts, we build up other people in the context of love. Unity in the body is built upon the exercise of these gifts. Each part contributes to the whole rather than duplicating the same gift.

Our gift (or gifts) indicates our primary ministry. When we are operating within the realm for which God has designed us, we gain a sense of being at home, an awareness of being in the right place. This was the case with one young woman I knew, who volunteered at a crisis pregnancy center. She'd had two abortions before she became a believer and knew firsthand the painful, long-term effects. Someone asked her why she enjoyed a ministry like this, one that was bound to produce discouraging results at times. She replied, "When I get to talk with these women about abortion, no matter what their response is, I feel like I am right where I ought to be. *I sense that this is what I was born to do.*"

That is exactly the feeling all of us need to look for in the exercise of our unique gifts in ministry—a sense of doing what we were "born for." Leaders should serve people in their ministry in order to bring them to this point. To ignore a believer's right fit in the body, and in a particular ministry, is the mark of a self-serving power leader.

WHEN LIMITATIONS ARE A GOOD THING

This moves us into a discussion about spheres of ministry. Whether one believes there are seven, twelve, twenty, or more valid gifts today is not as important as being aware that for each gift there are multiple kinds of service. And for each gift there are also multiple kinds of results (1 Corinthians 12:4-6).

While God has given a broad spectrum of spiritual gifts to build up the body of Christ, these gifts contain both closed doors and open avenues of service. As we begin to discover what our gifts are, we must also accept their limits.

One's gifting is innate and internal—it is what the Holy Spirit has uniquely bestowed upon a believer. The sphere of that gifting is more external—it is the capacity, or boundaries, in which the gift is best expressed. Paul appealed to his limits—or sphere—when he wrote to the Corinthians, "We will not boast beyond our measure, but within the measure of the sphere which God apportioned to us as a measure, to reach even as far as you" (2 Corinthians 10:13). While Paul exhorted us all to a life of faith, the gifts through which we exercise that faith, and the sphere in which we demonstrate them, will vary significantly with each individual.

Consider, for example, the gift of teaching. It can have a sphere of one-on-one, small-group, large-group, or mega-group teaching. One can serve as a gifted teacher on the printed page as a writer, over the airwaves as a radio Bible teacher, or in a face-to-face setting. Just because one has the gift of teaching does not mean the Spirit works in all teachers in each of these areas.

Some teachers operate best using a lecture method; others by using the events of life, as Jesus' teaching so often did. Some like topical teaching; others like expository teaching. Some prefer to use the synthesis approach—teaching the great overarching themes of the Bible. Still others can spend months on analysis, teaching a few paragraphs or chapters. Some teachers excel with different audiences, such as youth, collegians, single adults, baby boomers, or senior citizens. Other teachers can reach a broad spectrum of audiences in which God uses them to bear fruit.

All of these are spheres of ministry for the same gift. To insist that there is only one forum, one method, or one style in which a gift can work is to underplay the gifts in their manifold forms. New Testament believers openly acknowledged the limitations and diversity of their gifts and spheres. Peter knew that he was the apostle with the sphere of ministry to the Jews and not to the Gentiles. Paul, gifted in building foundations or "planting the seed," counted on Apollos and others to "water the seed" (1 Corinthians 3:5-6). These individuals practiced the freedom to specialize in particular arenas of service. And they depended solely upon God to supply the complementary gifts and resultant ministries needed. There was no imperative then, nor is there one now, to be omnicompetent supermen and superwomen.

What is the result when we do not acknowledge our limitations? First, it stands to reason that one member's disobedience to the proper stewardship of his gift will have a definite effect on the rest of the body. Failure to operate within our limits takes a physical, mental, emotional, and spiritual toll. When I tried to manage a conference facility rather than lead, teach, and innovate, I denied my own sphere of gifting. Part of me hated to admit that God had simply not called me to take on this type of task. It was tantamount to admitting that I was inadequate. As exhilarating as the illusion of omnicompetence was and is, it paled in comparison to the freedom born of humility that came with acknowledging that I was out of my sphere. The chest pains and burnout, the fatigue and lack of motivation—all disappeared when I stepped away from that situation.

Second, omnicompetence prevents the proper functioning of other members. I have discovered that living within the range of my gifts and limits fosters a deference to other members of the body that God intended all along. This type of deference provides others the opportunity to lead and develop. For example, I am not the one to manage a conference facility, but *as long as I occupied that spot, someone gifted to do it would never have the chance.*

Omnicompetence fosters pride and pretense, while living within our God-given boundaries makes room for interdependence among brothers and sisters in Christ. It is the same principle as obedience—living within God's laws is limiting, but those boundaries stake out the best kind of life for us. Gifting and spheres of ministry are sovereignly designed to glorify God through maximizing our contributions. They keep us on track, majoring in the things we are good at and minoring in the things we are not.

If all of these principles are true, then why do we live as though they are not? There are two primary reasons—pride and the quest for prominence and control. Writer Phillip Greenslade commented,

Paul wanted to reassure the Corinthians about himself and his team. "That we will not boast beyond our measure, but within the measure of the sphere which God had apportioned us." . . . In fact, our authority has greater weight, Paul says, because we are not overextending ourselves. Pressed to undertake commitments on every side, today's leaders would do well to take this to heart. Knowing our limitations is a saving grace.[2]

The more we live within our gifts and our spheres of ministry, the more we will see Christ manifested through the work of the Holy Spirit. In this way the grace of God spreads to others through us.

A FREEING RECOGNITION

The content of this chapter can be profoundly freeing to leaders and the people they serve. It removes the deception of indispensability from one's motivations and thinking. It's freeing to realize that the Head of the body designates to each of us the gifts and sphere of ministry for which we were designed.

If I live according to my limits, then I won't overestimate my importance or strive to be indispensable to those I'm serving. True humility forces us to admit our limits. We can ignore this truth through sin and dysfunction, but that will only bring hurt and damage to the body. The servant leader is willing to pray, "Lord, if you can't work *through* me, work *around* me."

It's through weaknesses, hurts, and limitations that God can use us in the development of others. In these areas, we are not able to compete for ministry; rather, we can step aside and allow others to develop.

If we are faithful stewards of our own gifts and spheres of ministry, we will probably be most comfortable serving God's people in a team context. Teams of leaders working together for the building up of God's people allow each leader to live most closely aligned to his or her gifting and sphere. Tasks and responsibilities are distributed around, with each person recognized for his or her unique contribution. The body is edified because all serve on a team. This is a model of ministry each believer can follow.

Even when vacancies scream to be filled, we must resist the tendency to fill them with any willing people who volunteer or by choosing who seem to be the most likely candidates. Getting the job done is not the key issue; that responsibility rests with the Lord. Our corporate faith will increase as we watch God raise up and place His man or woman in that position.

It will also force us to our knees to ask the Lord to provide just the right person, probably someone we never would have chosen on our own. After all, as Jim Petersen wrote in *Church Without Walls:*

> The history of the church, from God's perspective, is a history of the Holy Spirit using little people. It consists of a mustard seed here and there, some yeast hidden in dough, or a seed in the ground. Not many wise or influential people are included. Rather, it has been built upon the lowly. Most of these have lived and died unnoticed, probably feeling in their own hearts that they had never really accomplished much for God with their lives. This history we have lost, but not forever. We will no doubt hear it told us as we stand together before God's throne.[3]

REFLECT ON YOUR LEADERSHIP

- As thoroughly as you can, describe your spiritual gift(s) and your sphere of ministry.
- Think through the various ministries in which you've been involved: Where have these aligned with—and where have they diverged from—your gifts and sphere?
- Take a few minutes to dream: How could your gifts and sphere make the greatest contribution to the body? Where and how could you best do that?

- List several people you influence: What are some of their
  spiritual gifts? How can you serve and enable them to
  become more aligned with their gifts and sphere?

Respond to the Challenge

Cooperate with the Spirit by maximizing others' contributions to
kingdom work in the area of their gifts and spheres.

■ ■ ■

Thank You, Lord, for intricately designing each person and
using these personal blueprints to accomplish
Your desires.

9

LET MY PEOPLE GO!

Releasing God's People for Service

URING A SPAN OF FIVE SHORT YEARS, OVER FIFTEEN HUNDRED volunteers, from all walks of life, from all church backgrounds, and from several countries, have gone to sixty-three cities in eight countries of the former Soviet Union—each for a period of one year. Close to 95 percent of these folks never had formal missions training or vocational ministry experience. Yet they heard the call, raised the money, and went to spread the gospel.

In many cities in the early nineties they were the first foreigners to arrive with the gospel. As my friend Nelson Malwitz, founder of the Finisher's Second Career Missionary Movement, observed about these CoMissioners,

> Those who participated by donating a year's service, most all were people from the work place. . . . My observation was that these were not a collection of "poster people" but the Lord used the ordinary, the humble, to outperform the proud. If the Lord can use that bunch, he can use any. He only is looking for clean and available vessels.

For though the LORD is exalted, yet He regards the lowly;
but the haughty He knows from afar. (Psalm 138:6)

Just one practical example: Anita, an employee of a small business, could no longer live with the guilt of her immoral lifestyle.
She was deeply convicted by God, not in a church setting, but at
work. Some people at her company held a prayer meeting for
employees every Monday morning at 8:00 A.M. As Anita began to
pray, God showed her some changes she needed to make in her
life, leading to total transformation.

This prayer meeting was run by "untrained" people; they
simply wanted to represent Jesus to their fellow employees. These
are the people whom ministry leaders are called to equip for
kingdom work.

EQUIPPING THE PEOPLE OF GOD

Looking at the scene worldwide, we see that the believing community is growing fastest where there is ministry *of and by* the
people of God. The "unqualified" and "untrained" are being might-
ily used by the Holy Spirit because of their simple obedience to
His call for holiness, faith, and commitment.

In contrast, many churches and ministries in the United States
are built in part on a relatively small core group of "ministry professionals" who are committed to a particular vision. These individuals are much like the pillars of a North Carolina beach
house—remove even one of them and the entire structure is
severely weakened. Remove enough of them and the ministry itself
falls.

The fact that so many ministries depend upon the continuous
output of so few individuals is alarming. Kingdom ministry is
meant to be shared by each and every one of God's people. This
dependence on a few reveals that we have not released His people.
"Average" believers are not catching the vision of ministry. Why?

No doubt it has to do with our underlying idea of what constitutes a ministry and how these values, assumptions, and principles manifest themselves in our leadership practices and

structures. With rare exception, our models of leadership exclude the development of people. But as Christ's followers, we should be the ones leading in the field of people development. The Bible refers to this emphasis on people development as "equipping." Ephesians 4:11-12 provides the clearest directive on making this process a top priority for spiritual leaders. The team with which I've ministered calls it "Train-'n'-Release."

Releasing people for ministry requires trusting God and letting go of our tendency to hoard people for our own ministry agendas. If we define our area of responsibility as God's kingdom and not just as our own ministry, we are well on our way. But it's hard to do! Perhaps the question is whether we are willing to pray that God would raise up people through us, people who would far surpass us in their impact for Him, people whose impact might be in arenas we will never see. Perhaps their influence will not benefit our particular ministry agenda.

> *Perhaps the question is whether we are willing to pray that God would raise up people through us, people who would far surpass us in their impact for Him, people whose impact might be in arenas we will never see.*

To His disciples, Jesus said, "Beseech [pray to] the Lord of the harvest to send out laborers" (Luke 10:2). Indeed, any call to equip God's people must rest on His sovereign power in bringing people to labor in His fields. If we have an accurate vision of God, we learn to rest more peacefully in His provisions for recruiting, developing, and equipping His own people.

I have personally seen how God practices a "just-in-time" people management system. In a previous chapter, I introduced some of our team members to you. It looks easy on paper (and with five years of hindsight) to see what God did in bringing quality brothers and sisters to co-labor with me. At the time, though, I was dying under the workload—regularly putting in 100-hour work weeks, with little help and enormous needs facing me. I felt as though I had the weight of Russia on my back.

I cried out to the Lord for help, asking Him to provide the right people. For over two years after I took on that role, God systematically brought just the right people to make just the right contributions—just at the right time. Andria, Ralph, Bill, Myles, Eddie, Andy, and the rest came just as they were needed.

And as we began to downsize in some of our responsibilities, they would leave—just after they had made their primary contributions. I didn't understand this principle until after several years of watching God provide. He truly does practice just-in-time people management.

God will provide the right person exactly when that person is needed. But not before. When no one is available who is gifted or feels called to a particular needed task, we begin to pray, trusting God to provide. He does so at just the right time (which may not be our timing). Later we see God's wisdom and marvelous timing in giving us the right person in His own time.

With this in mind, let's look more closely at the process of equipping God's people as those just-in-time folks arrive on the scene. Here we'll focus on the resources, reasons, and principles for equipping.

RESOURCES FOR EQUIPPING GOD'S PEOPLE

As Paul makes clear in Romans, God is the one who saves and transforms. We are merely participants in His supernatural transformation process. Our rebirth is thoroughly supernatural, as will be our final translation at His appearing. It follows that the transformation process, taking us from spiritual infancy to full Christlike maturity, is also supernatural. Peter assures us that "His divine power has granted to us everything pertaining to life and godliness" (2 Peter 1:3). Paul exults that "We are His workmanship, created in Christ Jesus for good works, which God prepared beforehand, that we should walk in them" (Ephesians 2:10). Depending upon God's sufficiency, then, is the first prerequisite of developing people for kingdom service. Here's why.

God assumes the ultimate responsibility for developing people. This should be a tremendous relief to us. It can change our perspective from self-sufficiency to God's sovereignty. Our responsibility as equippers is not to change a believer's life; only the power of the Trinity can do that. Our obligation is to help believers focus on what the Father, Son, and Holy Spirit are doing in their lives, and on how to grow and minister according to God's unique design and calling. A major thrust of our equipping process is to encourage an authentic relationship and intimacy with God. Growth and ministry will then flow out of that authenticity.

Spiritual leadership is similar to being part of the "great cloud of witnesses" (Hebrews 12:1) who encourage, exhort, and exult as our fellow believers fix their eyes on the Author and Perfecter of our faith. It is not our great gifts, abilities, formulas, or sequential training plans that develop people.

God articulates His design for equipping in His written Word. The Word is powerful, a two-edged sword, the judge of the thoughts and intentions of the heart. As Paul said, it "is profitable for teaching, for reproof, for correction, for training in righteousness" for the man or woman of God (2 Timothy 3:16).

God told Hosea, "My people are destroyed for lack of knowledge" (Hosea 4:6). There would be a famine in the land for the words of the LORD, Amos predicted (see Amos 8:11). It's happening in our world today, isn't it? Despite the multitude of books, translations, commentaries, tapes, computer Bibles, and videos, believers are largely ignorant of life-giving spiritual truth. Equipping, then, must begin with a progressive study of the Word of God, moving steadily from milk to meat.

God gives multiple gifts to balance the equipping process. Worship, prayer, teaching, and sharing are just some of the functions that God wants exhibited in a community of believers. As an individual is exposed to the multiple gifts of the people of God, he will grow into a fuller understanding of who God is. As each individual member of the body is transformed more and more into the image of Christ, the whole body grows stronger.

REASONS FOR EQUIPPING GOD'S PEOPLE

Through the multiple gifts of the many, the Holy Spirit disciples and develops the one. Where one person cannot break through, another can. The result is the maturing of the body as a whole, and that is the prime reason for equipping every individual for ministry. But consider these other reasons.

Each individual believer has immense worth to God. Paul calls our attention to the incomparable truth that "God demonstrates His own love toward us, in that while we were yet sinners, Christ died for us" (Romans 5:8). This incredible fact rings throughout the Old Testament as well: "The LORD your God is in your midst. . . . He will exult over you with joy, He will be quiet in His love, He will rejoice over you with shouts of joy!" (Zephaniah 3:17). He redeems individuals to share in an eternity of glory and inheritance. We are priceless treasures in His eyes.

The ministry's burdens and blessings were meant to be shared by a joint priesthood. If we gathered any group of vocational ministry leaders in any room anywhere in the world, the topic of personal burnout, overwork, and lack of manpower would inevitably surface. God specifically raises up leaders to instruct the people in holy living and then to let them live it. He did not raise leaders to do the holy living *for* the people or to do the ministry *for* them. As leaders, we tend to hold to the doctrine of the priesthood of all believers even as we practice a "doctrine of the elite." The epidemic of ministry failure and burnout is perhaps a consequence of our unwillingness to apply the priesthood of every believer in the most practical ways.

The people of God collectively share responsibility for this situation. A group of believers who demand a shiny elite and productive leader to do *their* ministry and to run *their* organization as *they* want him to are headed for trouble. Leaders who try to correct this error sometimes find themselves out of a job. God intended ministry to be shared. Where this is not happening, it may be due to the hardheartedness of the people as much as to the ambition of a leader.

The identifying mark of a mature spiritual leader is his or her desire to develop the next generation of believers and leaders. This is an individual who practices the John the Baptist philosophy: He or she consciously chooses to decrease so that another may increase. He or she makes an effort to steer his disciples to others who will continue the process.

When leading seminars with ministry leaders, I ask them to list the elements of ministry. Usually at the top of their lists is the ministry of preaching and teaching the Word. Then I ask, "Are you equipping the laity to do that ministry? Do you equip them to preach and teach?" The typical response is silence. If we are not equipping people for *all* of the ministry, including our own jobs, then do we really believe in the priesthood of believers?

The people of God gathered will not reach the world. Only the people of God *scattered* can do it. "As you go, make disciples of all nations . . ." are Jesus' words. The first-century apostles and believers practiced this commandment. The world was turned upside down, not because Paul was a great preacher using mass media techniques to reach the millions, but because he and others trained and developed people who, in turn, went out among the lost throughout the known world. In every walk of society they spoke of Christ, and many, many people "were added to the Lord."

Jesus and the apostles modeled a Train-'n'-Release ministry style. Jesus' development of the Twelve was one of His primary ministry goals.[1] The original disciples, in turn, developed others. By the time we finish reading Acts, we see a huge network of leaders moving among the local fellowships. They were constantly training, developing, encouraging, and teaching others.

PRINCIPLES FOR EQUIPPING GOD'S PEOPLE

Now that we've looked at some of the resources and reasons for equipping people to serve, let's summarize the process itself with a few general principles.

The process must cooperate with God's unique design for each believer. C. S. Lewis once said that when an individual was wholly God's he would be more himself than ever before. In that incredible statement he captured the essence of why any equipping process must respect the uniqueness of the individual. People don't come to us as blank slates upon which we write whatever we need them to be at the moment.

Each person is the creation of a painstaking Designer. Our

role is to cooperate with the Holy Spirit in people's lives as the
Master seeks to free them to become more and more of who they
truly are. God has a purpose and a plan for each of His children
that in some mysterious way fulfills a larger plan than any one of
us can grasp.

Servant leaders, therefore, seek to maximize each individual.
My questions regarding those whom I serve are, How can I cooperate with the way the Holy Spirit has gifted them? What is He
doing in their lives? How can I assist them with that process?

I have a friend who easily designs new ways of doing ministry
and skillfully writes curriculum. But he wilts under the pressure
of operating a ministry day in and day out. He sees his contribution as being in the design phase and is content to trust God for
the strength and patience to do just that.

*The process must enable the people of God to minister as a
community and not simply as individuals.* God sovereignly chose
the word pictures of a bride and groom, a body, and a kingdom to
communicate His desire that His people be a unified presence in
the world. We are a part of each other; there is no such thing as a
"Lone Ranger" believer. God's people grow, minister, and develop
in the context of community. An equipping process should involve
helping people grow in their relational abilities as they learn to minister together as a team. They need to see that the quality of their
relationships is as much a ministry and a witness to the world as
the actual work they are trying to accomplish.

*The process of equipping the saints is done among, and for the
sake of, the lost.* We equip the saints in order to help them live *in
the world* as salt and light. In this way, the lost have their appetites
whetted for the Lord. We do not develop people for their own ful-
fillment (or ours). Our aim must go deeper than producing the
most polished presentations, as though the world would find us
legitimate only if we spoke their language and gave an appearance
of being upbeat and trendy. The world is hungry for depth, substance, and true character—genuine evidence of the gospel taking root in human lives.

As leaders, we must commit ourselves to our own and others'
ongoing spiritual development. We must candidly confront the

behavioral and cultural standards we have falsely presented as the marks of a follower of Jesus. Then we must courageously commit ourselves to God's estimation of true disciples of Jesus: those who manifest sacrifice, character, and obedience. Only the greater calling of reaching the lost will draw the diverse members of the body together.

Most ministries today practice a congenial competition. While they mouth words of unity, there is little practical action to back up their pronouncements. Their real goal is to accumulate members in their ministry organization or church while the lost still await the good news from a unified body of Christ. A student ministry worker relayed to me his frustration in this regard:

> Jack was on staff with another student ministry, and he was very agreeable to meeting with me when I called. I wanted to discuss two matters with him. One was the issue of our groups competing to recruit the same people. The other was the matter of confusion among many unbelievers as to why committed Christians in different groups did not display much unity. I said, "Jack, we sometimes recommend that Christian students we meet would do better by being involved with your group. Do you ever encourage students to get involved with our group instead of your own?"
>
> He responded along these lines: "We're trying to generate a movement, and we need everyone involved with us. Besides, we feel that we can meet a very broad spectrum of needs as well as anyone else."
>
> I felt his response reflected arrogance. He seemed to feel that he and his group had a corner on the truth, and he clearly didn't recognize the unique contributions of other student ministries.
>
> My second issue—of having joint activities to increase our effectiveness and to display our unity to a watching world—received a similar response. Jack felt that things would be better if we went our own separate ways. Yet I am still distressed by the signals that these

fragmented approaches send out to unbelievers.

HOW FREEDOM CAN LOOK

Releasing God's people—giving them the freedom to be and to serve as God intended—is freeing for leaders themselves. The body was meant to grow as each part does its work, not just as the leaders do the work. God does indeed have a master plan for multiplying our efforts through all of His people.

I have been part of numerous ministries in which training and equipping for ministry have been at the heart of what we do. Only as I surround myself with people who complement and balance my gifts do we really provide a quality equipping process. We work together as a team of partners with a common heart and vision— the process of training and releasing people for ministry.

On one of our first CoMission teams to go to Russia, a fifty-year-old volunteer had never done any personal ministry. But now he had committed to minister in Russia for a year. After our two weeks of intensive training, followed by six weeks of ongoing development in Russia, he began—slowly at first, and then within several months—to see former atheists come to Christ.

After ten months in the country, he had this to say about the experience:

> The CoMission team of trainers worked together to pro-
> vide perspectives, concepts, and skills for our ministry in
> Russia. Then they had the confidence to send us out as a
> team to the field with a clear process and a training man-
> ual. God used our lives beyond our wildest expectations
> here in Russia. We now have confidence that God will use
> our lives back in the States. We are committed and believe
> we can reach our neighbors for Christ because we saw it
> happen here.

I remember a time early in our ministry in Russia. I led a week-long training conference in Moscow. I will never forget this big guy—at least 6' 4" and 250 pounds. He was standing behind several people, waiting to talk with me after one of my training sessions. When it was his turn, he came up to me with tears running down his cheeks and blurted out with sobs, "Thank you, thank you for helping me, a truck driver, become successful in ministry to the Russians. . . . (pause, with sobs) I never thought this could happen. . . . I didn't think I could do it. . . . I've never been to college or Bible school. . . . I came to help . . . but God has made me fruitful with the Russian teachers!" (By now a smile began to form on his face, but the tears of joy still streamed down his cheeks.) "Thank you for your training because this has shown me that I, even I, can do it. And I am doing it. I am ministering to these Russians!"

That's the freedom for ministry that equipping brings. And freedom for the people we train is best modeled in the ways we leaders and colleagues relate together. We are a team of co-equals, each with a different set of gifts and callings, each with a particular contribution to make. We make our contribution and then step back to allow another to do the same. This modeling of group ministry in action speaks volumes more than all the lectures or seminars we could provide.

Yet, it's important to remember that an equipping ministry will begin slowly. As it develops, it will create extensive participation. The tasks at hand may often take a backseat to the more crucial task: developing intimate involvement with other believers. Ultimately, the result will be that more and more believers begin to envision a personal ministry niche that reflects their gifts and calling in the body.

A close friend of mine ministered in a college-town church in Oklahoma. The church never grew beyond eighty or ninety people at one time—never a significant church in terms of size. But it had a significant ministry in terms of equipping and developing people. As college students came through and attended, they were built up, equipped, and developed. After graduation, some went to seminary, others to the mission field or into careers where they still walk with God. These students got their start, their heart for ministry and their initial equipping, through my friend's ministry. And that ministry has had a continuing impact in many parts of the country and world. Equipping pays off for the kingdom if not in our organization. After all, whose kingdom are we serving—ours or His?

There is less and less tolerance in our society for the basic tenets of the Bible. Humanism, pragmatism, and relativism hold sway. Respect toward divine, objective truth is wearing thin. Because of these trends, God's people may well be in for a season of unprecedented persecution. When our lives are on the line, all our organizational distinctives, high-powered programs, or church traditions will mean little, if anything. Only a community of deeply committed men and women can persevere. It will be a group of wounded healers, nourished on the Word of God, focused on the Author and Perfecter of their faith, and aware of the transient nature of this world.

> *Equipping pays off for the kingdom if not in our organization. After all, whose kingdom are we serving—ours or His?*

If the church is the body, the holy presence of Christ in the world, its most fundamental task is to build communities of holy character. And the first priority of those communities is to disciple men and women to maturity in Christ and then equip them to live their faith in every aspect of life and in every part of the world.[2]

■

REFLECT ON YOUR LEADERSHIP

Analyze the equipping processes used in your ministry by asking yourself these questions:

- What is our overall plan used in equipping people? What vision, outcome, or agenda drives the equipping process? Who is being equipped?
- For what areas of ministry are people being equipped? Is everyone's gift being used and developed?
- Who is doing a particularly good job of releasing God's people for ministry in my city? Why do I think

they're doing a good job? What can I learn and apply from my observations?

Respond to the Challenge

Seek to free people from limiting agendas in order to prepare them for the greatest freedom: serving kingdom goals.

■ ■ ■

Lord, I want to yield myself to Your vision for my ministry. Help me to set Your people free so they can fulfill all You desire for them, to Your glory.

10

HOW WILL YOU UNLEASH THEM?

Leading Releasing Systems and Structures

THERE WERE HUNDREDS OF CANDLES BURNING WITH A SHIMMERING, dancing light on ceilings and walls, and the powerful smell of incense mixed with the fragrant aroma of hot wax pervaded the air. It was overwhelming and awe-inspiring!

As I walked through the back of the old Russian Orthodox Church, people were praying before beautifully painted icons of Jesus, Mary, and the apostles. Some were kissing these icons. I heard monotone chanting reverberating in the rafters.

As I moved toward the front of the church a new sense of awe came over me as I caught glimpses of the bearded priests. They wore flowing white robes with ornate gold and multicolored belts and necklaces, huge crosses swinging from their necks. Then my eyes lifted toward the heavenlies as I looked upward inside the onion-shaped dome. Gold was everywhere, and the paintings reflected the work of reverent, masterful artists.

Toward the front of the church was a tall, ornate false front of gold with beautiful yet subdued paintings; little alcoves for icons and burning incense, and other symbols. As the service progressed, beautiful antiphonal singing embraced my attention. It was a cappella, and the four-part harmony echoed throughout the church. The priests performed ceremonies I didn't understand as they worshiped God, acting as intermediaries between the standing people and the awesome yet removed God.

I stood transfixed in the cold, damp building, trying to keep my hands warm in my pockets. All of the women had scarves covering their heads. The scarves were interesting, and each reflected the apparent economic status of the women. Some of the head coverings were ragged; some were of fine material. I also saw seven or eight women for every man there. Even at that, most were older men or young boys.

Just then an old woman came over to me and said something in harsh words that I didn't understand. I looked to my Russian interpreter for help. "What did she say?" I whispered.

"She said, 'Take your hands out of your pockets!'" Then he explained in a whisper, "The Russians view that as disrespectful."

This snapped me back into a rational frame of mind. I began thinking, "Wow, this is what it must have been like a thousand years ago!" Then I leaned against one of the big pillars holding up the building. (We had been standing for a long time, and I thought this could give my back a rest.) As I leaned there, I saw an old man work his way past me. He had not taken a bath for a long time and hadn't shaved for several days. He glanced at me and probably knew instantly that I was a foreigner by my glasses and haircut. He smiled at me — one of the few smiles voluntarily given by a stranger. He was an old man with some military medals pinned over his heart on a ragged old coat. His smile revealed several missing teeth, and of the ones that remained, several gold.

My interpreter leaned over to me again. He said, "The Russians are offended by leaning against the post."

When Forms Become Sacred

Ever since the former Soviet Union opened its doors to outsiders, many Westerners have had the opportunity to worship in a Russian Orthodox church. It is a truly unforgettable, rich experience. And it is exactly how the gospel was introduced in tenth-century

Russia. The church service was designed to communicate the great truths of sin and redemption, suffering and resurrection to a population consisting largely of illiterate peasants. Since few people could read, they *experienced* the message with all their senses through colorful imagery and liturgical drama.

The church remains today, a thousand years later, essentially in its original form. Yet the Russian peasantry has evolved into a highly literate nation where even a taxi driver can discuss Dostoyevski like a literature professor. The average Russian asks deep, penetrating questions about the nature and meaning of life — questions that the gospel uniquely addresses. But he typically hasn't looked to the Orthodox Church for guidance or answers in the last century. The church is perceived as being irrelevant and out of touch. In all its elaborate decoration and ceremony, it is cut off from the average person. One Russian recently told me, "Every time I'm in church, I feel like I'm just a piece of sand."

The Russian Orthodox service is a classic example of how easily form can supplant function. But this pattern is by no means unique to any one culture or group of people; it is endemic to human nature. Yet the New Testament gives us the freedom to question such established forms because it makes only the essentials — God and His Word — holy. Systems and structures are human inventions to further divine ends. They are not sacred in themselves; they are expendable. Even Sunday school can be rethought.

We, of all people, have freedom to ask the hard questions. Is this procedure, this organization, this service, or this program really accomplishing the most desirable ends? Is there a better way? Are we applying our standard form to whatever the need might be? Are we being called to risk creating something new? What form will better enable people to grow in Christ? What will further the kingdom? What will further the equipping of God's people and release them for ministry?

Asking such questions will help us create "releasing structures" that move people into ministry under the guidance of the Holy Spirit. What would these structures be like? Consider three characteristics.

Releasing Structures Enhance Relationships

When we think of structure, even the invisible spiritual variety, we normally think in terms of a straight, linear design. Every effect has a cause, with every action leading to a predictable reaction. But the basis of a structure that serves people and enables them to grow is a *relational* one. Its form should be that of a living organism, not a static or necessarily linear one. The design resembles a matrix, an interweaving together of individual lives into a rich tapestry of truth and love.

Scripture uses two primary images to describe the relationships operating in God's kingdom: the body and the family. The human body is a complex organism whose life and outward motions result from the working together of many small parts, some of those quite hidden and humble. Similarly, the body of Christ exists in relationships built upon interdependence, the working together of many interwoven parts. There are many parts but one body. These relationships of interdependence—with each other in the Lord—are the foundational dynamic of kingdom life. And as the word *dynamic* implies, their life-giving quality comes from a recognition that relationships flourish in an atmosphere of freedom. In this environment, people nurture and challenge each other in the real and raw places of life.

> *Relationships are not a matter of mere convenience or a triviality that God superimposes on His children. Rather they are essential to life, particularly life in the kingdom. . . .*

Our relationships as believers also resemble a family, which originates in the interaction among the Father, the Son, and the Holy Spirit. All of life flows out of the relationships existing within the Trinity. *This is why we can say that the essence of life is relational.* Relationships are not a matter of mere convenience or a triviality that God superimposes on His children. Rather they are essential to life, particularly life in the kingdom, because of the love of the Father for His Son and Their desire that we share in that love.

A closer look at the relationships within the Trinity is like gazing on a masterpiece of interdependence. The Father claims that

He loves the Son and has given all things into His hand. But the Son insists that He does not act on His own; He can do nothing unless His Father bids it. The Son does what is pleasing to the Father and revels not in His own glory but in the glory the Father gives Him.

The Son says plainly that He must leave [earth] because otherwise we would not be able to appreciate the work of the third member of the Trinity, the Holy Spirit. He, too, must play His part. He came to reveal and glorify the Son, and to convict and draw people into relationship with the Father and the Son. Why does this relational drama take place? So that we might be invited into the very center of the love of the Trinity. Thus Jesus prays to the Father "that the love you have for me may be in them and that I myself may be in them" (John 17:26, NIV).

Relationships, then, are the true underpinnings of any releasing structure. They are the heart and soul of spiritual life—of life in the kingdom. And while we fail to love perfectly, our relationships are meant to be marked by the very qualities we see in the Trinity—honor, mutual respect, deference, and a willingness to expend ourselves for the good of another brother or sister in Christ.

While each member of the family of Christ has his or her specific roles to play in accomplishing kingdom purposes, the relationships among its members are critically important. Those relationships do not emphasize rank. Instead, we stand shoulder to shoulder, mutually supporting and deferring to one another. We step up to make our contribution and then step back into our place to encourage and applaud the contribution of others. Robert Banks explains that in the early church, distinctions among individuals were not the means by which "some maintained an advantage over others, but instead . . . the means by which some had the opportunity to serve others."[1]

The primary mark of relationships among individuals in the body is love. In fact, love is such a preeminent virtue that Christ gives the onlooking world the right to judge our spirituality based on the quality of love they observe. "By this all men will know that you are my disciples, if you love one another" (John 13:35, NIV).

Enabling such a sense of community must be a primary

concern, so that the environments and structures we help to create as leaders really do further relationships within the body. In
so doing, the onlooking world is invited into a circle of warmth
and light. The organization should exist to serve this dynamic
organism.

Releasing Structures Are Built Around the Spirit's Leadership

At Pentecost every believer became a priest to the community of
God. Individuals, filled with the person of the Holy Spirit, were
given a particular spiritual gift. These gifts were distributed to
enable the priesthood to minister to both the saved and the lost
as the new corporate body of the Lord Jesus.

The Holy Spirit is our Teacher, Comforter, and Counselor as
we grow in the walk of faith. As God, He alone knows exactly
what a local community of believers needs for spiritual nourish-
ment and so orders the proper balance of His gifts within that
body. Their fellowship, and all that results from it, is not a human
work but a divine gift.

A reasonable question at this point would be: If we depend
upon the Holy Spirit for the proper structure for any given gath-
ering, could this not lead to confusion at best and imbalance at
worst? The answer is no.

> The character of the Spirit does not allow this to happen.
> He acts as the agent of a God who is "not a God of confu-
> sion but of peace" (1 Corinthians 14:33). His sovereignty
> over the gifts results in a relatively stable, though not
> inflexible, distribution within the community. . . . Each
> gathering of the community will have its structure, but
> that will emerge naturally from the particular combination
> of the gifts that comes to expression in it and the order in
> which they are exercised.[2]

The community's part in the Spirit's work is to be available,
humble, and sensitive to His leading. True to His nature, the Holy
Spirit will not violate a person's will in order to accomplish His

mission, so availability is a choice each of us must make. An attitude of humility is also essential to a servant structure. Even as pride demands the best seat in the house, humility in turn relinquishes all rights, allowing Christ to be all and in all (Colossians 3:11), and submits to the gifting of others.

How do we become sensitive to the leading of the Spirit? It comes when we learn to tune out the cacophony of conflicting demands—of self and others—and simply listen for His still, small voice to speak. What freedom it brings!

It must grieve the Spirit to see us looking to the past, grasping for stale words and worn-out procedures to carry out His work. He must be appalled to see us focusing on buildings and programs rather than clinging to the life of Christ within us, which can so capably move us out into the world in fresh, anointed power. Indeed, the central message of the gospel is that He came to indwell us, empower us, and send us out as His royal priesthood with a ministry of reconciliation.

Releasing Structures Rely on Shared Leadership

Shared leadership is a must for a truly enabling environment. I believe it can happen in a variety of ways and settings. The ministry organizational chart doesn't determine its feasibility; the heart, humility, and mind-set of the organization's leaders does that. In most ministries, one person usually has the final say on certain matters, and that isn't necessarily right or wrong. Rather, the issue is: Does this person glean spiritual wisdom from others and thus *share the leadership* in his or her area of responsibility?

My experience has taught me that a team approach works best when leading a ministry. A few years ago I was "the leader" whose name was attached to the bottom line. In reality, I didn't lead that large ministry by myself. When it came to the operation of our twenty-plus annual training conferences in the United States and in the former Soviet Union, there were people far more competent than I. So I submitted to their leadership in the areas of their gifting. When it came to designing our training curricula, I followed the leadership of my colleagues who were gifted in a particular area, such as Bible exposition, team building, communication, and so on. In fact, each member of our team of equippers had certain areas of expertise in which they led the others. Even though the organization I ministered with held me accountable for what was going on, I trusted God to lead us by means of the gifts He had given to all of us.

I learned a powerful lesson in that shared approach to leadership: God does more through our cooperative efforts as fellow leaders than any one of us (including me) could do individually. I have also learned that God uses a dynamic, participatory, cooperative environment to generate ideas and ministry outcomes that we as leaders could never produce alone. Within this arena of mutual involvement, God's Spirit has fresh opportunity to work through all of the people and elements involved. Greater participation and responsibility deepen a sense of ownership and shared leadership, which in turn leads to greater commitment and willingness to sacrifice for one another. All of this makes the releasing ministry easier.

Structures that are truly equipping are fluid structures, and they allow for a continuously changing dynamic and the growth of God's people. Leaders, then, view equipping and discipling processes as just that — *processes* that are evolving and responsive to the needs of those being served. The processes are not policies. Otherwise, ministry systems and structures block and hinder the real ministry in people's lives. Structures and systems should always be malleable tools used for the benefit of those they were designed to serve.

A releasing ministry structure is the best means of allowing God's work to happen in peoples' lives. Servant systems and structures facilitate real ministry. They exist to serve and are only a means, never an end. The greatest favor we can do for one another is to occasionally challenge the existence and effectiveness of the structures in which we operate. To do that, which question would you ask first?

■

REFLECT ON YOUR LEADERSHIP

- What would it take to change the structure of your ministry? What is the likelihood it *could* change? Why?
- Make a list of your unique "spiritual gift mix." What kind of structure would truly enable you to use these gifts in ministry? What would help enable the people you serve?
- What are some forms, traditions, or programs in your ministry that seem to resist change? Why are they so resistant?
- As you think through your leadership style (or consider the leaders you know), how can you better use structures and forms to serve people?

Respond to the Challenge

Establish a releasing environment that will provide freedom and support for God's people to respond to His Spirit's leading, individually and corporately.

■ ■ ■

By Your strength, Father, I want to help re-form an environment where Your people can flourish beyond anything I have seen before.

11

FAITH AND COURAGE
Leading from a Posture of Humble Strength

IN A QUIET ROOM ABOVE SOME COMMON LIVING QUARTERS, THE DIS-
ciples gathered with Jesus to celebrate the Passover. Everything
was prepared, and an air of expectancy hung over the pro-
ceedings. Perhaps now, finally, Jesus would make public what His
disciples felt had to be the truth. He was no ordinary man. His
true identity as the Messiah had been veiled in parable and innu-
endo far too long. Maybe now the truth would be spoken aloud.
Then Jesus and His disciples would be ushered into the pinnacle
of influence and power. As His closest associates, had they not
proved their worth and competence?

With amazement Christ's disciples watched as their Master
stood and took off His outer garment. He laid aside His dignity.
What kind of king is this? they must have thought. They watched
Him pour water into a basin, tie a towel about His waist, and
kneel before them. Like a common servant, He intended to wash
their feet. They looked down into His eyes as He stooped to
serve them.

And Peter, as always, was the one to say what everyone else
was thinking. "Lord, surely you can't mean to wash my feet?"

TEMPTED TO DO OTHERWISE

This scene ranks as one of the most significant in Christ's ministry. It was His last evening with His disciples—His friends. His death was imminent. "When a man knows the end is near, only the important surfaces. Impending death distills the vital. The trivial is bypassed. The unnecessary is overlooked. That which is vital remains."[1] In these last hours, Jesus' vital choice was to exercise His authority and power . . . as a servant.

As the rest of the story of the early church unfolds, it is clear that Christ's disciples eventually understood the significance of the leader-as-servant message. He was able to embrace the posture of a servant because He knew He belonged to the Father. Therein lay His security; He had nothing to prove. Those last few hours with His disciples could have been devoted to many worthwhile goals. Yet, the eloquent message Christ left with His disciples was to model the role of servant.

There will always be temptation to do it otherwise. Leaders, especially spiritual leaders, change, grow, and evolve over time. Leadership isn't like a trip through western Kansas that covers miles and miles of the same flat prairie land, where every hour looks to be a repeat of the one before. The scenery of leadership is constantly changing. New opportunities and new temptations appear at every turn, and we either grow or wither with the journey.

In the realm of spiritual leadership, as soon as we begin to feel we've "made it," we're probably in trouble. If we want to become— and remain—servant leaders throughout our lives, we must be able to identify the obstacles in our path. There will always be pressures to lead out of our natural, fleshly capacity. Those pressures come in many forms, but let's consider three of the hardest pressures to withstand.

1. Pressure: When your identity as a leader becomes fused with your ministry. Over the course of our lives, there must always be a clear distinction between "the ministry" and "ourselves." We are to stand as men and women before the Lord, who loves us as His very own sons and daughters. Whatever ministry God gives us is always secondary to that reality. Our ministry flows out of the experience of being divinely His. When our identity as a leader becomes fused with our ministry, then any challenge or criticism will feel quite personal—an attack on who we are. It's *me* who feels threatened. If we are so heavily invested in the ministry, then we won't be able to let go, won't be able to separate self from work. Our very life feels at stake.

When this happens, we inhibit the freedom to allow something new to happen, to allow a ministry to take a different shape. We begin to subtly require a blind loyalty from people, one that defers to our desires and plans, because we are "the leader."

The true nature of life and ministry is an ebb and flow. The structure and forms change constantly as people develop and their needs evolve. This reality requires that, as leaders, we stay flexible and adaptable, able to let go when needed. We must hold our ministry with an open hand, or we will squeeze out its very life. If our identity becomes confused with our position or responsibility as a leader, we will then leave behind our calling to be a servant.

I have faced this kind of temptation in my own ministry. For several years it had been a fast-paced collage of planning and activity in leading a team of dedicated trainers and equippers. Together we had given ourselves to preparing hundreds of men and women for a year of ministry inside the former Soviet Union. More than any other, this ministry was the right fit for my own preparation and gifting. My natural inclination was to want to keep everything just as it was and to protect my position as a leader.

Like so many true ministries, this program was designed to meet a specific need at a specific time. When first asked to do the training, we team members allowed ourselves five years to make a strategic contribution. Then we would reevaluate. As I look back, I realize more than ever that I couldn't afford to allow my identity as a servant to become one with the ministry I was leading. I couldn't grow so comfortable and attached to the ministry as it was that when change was needed and desirable, I would stand in the way.

I know if I approach leadership in any other way, I cannot be a servant of those I'm committed to equip. If my identity is fused with the ministry I'm leading, I will be a roadblock to the greater purposes of God.

2. Pressure: When "the organization" begins to take on a life of its own. Like the steady shifting motion of the continental shelf, every organization drifts toward perpetuating itself. Religious enterprises are no exception. What often begins as a pioneering effort, held together by faith, prayer, and a little planning, will tend toward becoming an institution, once it finds a measure of success. In the process, the real ministry agenda shifts toward maintenance.

How does this natural process affect us as leaders who desire to be servants? It means that we must stay sensitive to our true goals. We must be careful not to fall into the trap of looking to any human ministry organization—whether a church or parachurch—as a father figure to give us security or significance. No one can provide us with a truly safe harbor except the Lord.

Ministry organizations, at their best, are always meant to serve. Our job as a leader is to make sure they do.

C. S. Lewis once said that "the fatal tendency in all human activity is for the means to encroach upon the very ends" for which they were intended. Spiritual leaders are the ones responsible for asking the hard questions that will keep an organization sensitive to the real needs of people. They should be guardians, not of an institution or ministry organization, but of those being served and of the Lord's purposes. The organization itself shouldn't become the fiddler who plays the music to which everyone must dance.

3. Pressure: When people demand a leader who will think and choose for them. Part of the pressure to lead from a position of authority and control comes from the very people we are meant to serve. All of us, at one time or another, will run into the same human cry that Samuel heard in the day of the judges. "Give us a king!" the people demanded (1 Samuel 8:5-6). God was the one who *was* their King, but the Israelites insisted they must have someone in the flesh.

That cry still rings out today. People gravitate toward a human personality in whom they can put their trust. It's easier that way. They assume a pseudo parent-child relationship with a leader who will think and choose for them. This is the motivation behind that common tendency to "put someone on a pedestal." If we can convince ourselves that a leader is not like us—human, flawed, dependent on God and others—then we can follow his vision without stopping to wait on the Lord ourselves.

If we allow others to place us in this untouchable category as a leader, to make us the final word, we will do both them and ourselves a great disservice. The ministry becomes a crushing burden when it ultimately rests upon one person. Though initially attractive, being made the leader in this sense leaves you isolated and alone, cut off from the rest of the body—the ones who can provide the fellowship and accountability a leader needs.

The choice is really ours. Will we allow others to exalt us according to human standards? Or will we let God exalt us in His time and according to His standards? The answer is crucial. Leaders are susceptible to pride, yet God is opposed to the proud. We need to ask ourselves: Will I accept the praise of human beings or of God? If we do things for the praise of men, we already have our reward in full. Or do we believe God's Word to be true—that He will raise up the humble in due time?

In the final analysis, allowing people to make us "the leader" is a denial of the truth that Jesus Himself is the Head of the body. If we usurp His role, do we not become, in practice, a pseudo deity? Yet only He can lead an individual or a group of people in the way they are meant to go. As we serve the Lord, we help to strengthen the spiritual muscles in people so that they rely on Him with greater faith and vision.

CHECKPOINTS ALONG THE WAY

Paul said in his letter to Timothy that for some of us our sins are quite evident; they precede us. But for others, their sins follow after them and are not so apparent (1 Timothy 5:24). In regard to servant leadership, we find that the real issues we face over the long haul are matters of the heart. Solomon's heart, for example, was led astray by his many wives (1 Kings 11:3). Today's leaders, in the same way, can be led astray by the exaltation that comes from many followers.

The desire to be a servant leader should cause us to examine our hearts and our motivations, no matter what the size or extent of our ministry. We can do it by constantly asking ourselves several tough questions.

Is Jesus Christ the focus of attention around here? There is an old saying that "Jesus will be central." It doesn't matter what else we lift up in His place, it will always fail us or fall short, and we will be led, time and again, back to acknowledging His supremacy in our lives. Nothing can fill His place. As servant leaders, we want to stay as close as possible to that fundamental truth.

If we keep Christ central, then our plans, programs, and personalities will not be the spotlight of our ministry. Building an organization, or physical facilities, or self-image cannot be the focus of our passion and excitement. After all, have we really accomplished something great just because our ministry has grown? Isn't the real barometer of value the quality of our worship? Are our hearts being turned to the Lord in deeper devotion?

Are relationships the lifeblood of this ministry? Christ said the world would recognize us as being His by the way we treat one another. Even as I write those words, I am convicted by their simple clarity and weightiness. Christ places such an emphasis on our relationships with one another that He makes them the litmus test of true spirituality. It is amazing and challenging. Clearly, He meant for our relationship to each other, and our willingness to serve each other, to be the greatest apologetic around.

Building authentic community in the life of the body is not an addendum to the ministry; it is not something we hope will happen when there is time and energy available. Rather, it is the lifeblood of our ministry. If depth and authenticity in relationships are key concerns for us, then pride and ambition will be seen as the roadblocks they are. Biblical relationships are built on humility, transparency, and growing intimacy with one another and the Lord.

We must come to prize people in the way that God does— desiring their best interests, seeing them as individuals, yet remaining unwilling to minimize their sin. If this is our focus, then our ministry structures will reflect that perspective. Rather than using people to accomplish the objectives we have in mind, we will serve them as a way of serving Christ.

Can I let go of control and step aside when I need to? As we move further into ministry, it's important to know where, and under what conditions, we are most prone to seek to control circumstances, results, and people.

I have discovered, for instance, that the most vulnerable chink in my armor is in the realm of concepts and ideas. This is where I am most tempted to say, "My way is the right way. I know it is. And if you'll listen to me long enough, you'll know it, too." I become fused with my ideas and it's difficult to separate criticism of the idea from criticism of me. When it comes to the conceptual underpinnings of a particular ministry initiative, it's hard for me to be flexible, to really listen. In short, it's difficult for me to trust God and let go of the need to control the outcome.

> *So much of ministry is the repeated exercise of beginning something, watching others grow and develop, and then letting go. If we don't counteract our need to control, we will find it difficult to fulfill one of our central callings as a leader: to give away the ministry.*

The inordinate tendency to control manifests itself differently for each of us, according to our makeup and gifting. For some, the hot buttons revolve around issues like finances, or correct appearances, or personnel matters. In whatever way these issues of control surface, they are like small grenades, holding the potential to destroy real ministry and relationships. For each of us, they represent the antithesis of trusting God as the One in control.

So much of ministry is the repeated exercise of beginning something, watching others grow and develop, and then letting go. If we don't counteract our need to control, we will find it difficult to fulfill one of our central callings as a leader: to give away the ministry.

Am I growing more conscious of my leadership values and assumptions? The only way we can lead from a spiritual and biblical basis is to continually evaluate *why we do what we do* and then measure our responses by the Scriptures. What values and assumptions underlie this ministry? How do we define success? What criteria indicate genuine growth and maturing in the life of those we serve? These are some of the questions that will lead us to evaluate biblically.

Looking at leadership and ministry in this way will steer us away from excessive pragmatism. Trusted methods and techniques may work well, but when we rely solely on them, they turn into tyrants. If success must be measured by numbers and size, we will forever be the prisoner of those things that make us feel like successful, effective leaders. In a real sense, only God can be trusted. Evaluating the values and assumptions of our leadership model means that substance, not just appearance, becomes the key concern.

What kind of change agent am I? A pastor once told me about a ninety-six-year-old woman in his church who one day summarized for him how many people secretly view change in ministries. "What I love about this church," she told him, "is that it's just exactly like it was when I first came here at the age of eight." In eighty-eight years hardly anything had changed!

While the fundamentals of the faith are indeed changeless, the external trappings and comfortable forms of conveying its truth should be in flux with every generation. Form must fit function, thereby meeting the reality of changing needs. Indeed, some elements of change lie at the heart of the message of the gospel. God calls us to ongoing repentance (which literally means "a change of mind") that is both personal and corporate.

Becoming redemptive agents of transformation is an essential part of our calling. Change requires a humility of spirit and a willingness to take risks with the unknown and the unfamiliar. To risk is to admit that the possibility of failure is real. It is also a willingness to let go of familiar forms and standards of success. Without openness toward change, we'll be ninety-six years old and still hanging on to whatever reminds us of the good ol' days.

God uses a few particular spiritual gifts in His body as agents of change. The gifts of apostle and prophet are two of those agents. People with apostolic gifts are given to the body to pioneer, steer, correct, and point the direction in which we need to go. Ministries, particularly large ones, need to have apostles leading them or, at a minimum, influencing them in a broad way from a distance.

> The foundation-laying ministry of apostles is essential if churches undergoing radical change are to come onto clear ground and those wholly new groupings of God's people are to come onto a secure and biblical basis. . . . It goes without saying that we need such [people] today.[2]

A prophet has unusual ability to clarify the issues and bring the truth to bear in the places we need it. It's important to recognize those whom God has gifted in this capacity, so we can heed them and move in fruitful directions.

Our basis for leadership must be correct:
- NOT power positions
  - NOT power control
    - NOT power people
      - NOT power structures
BUT a powerful God who works through us on His terms!

Up to this point, we have polarized two contrasting concepts of leadership—power leadership and servant leadership—which have been active throughout the history of God's people. This polarization is necessary if we are to become clear about what is spiritual leadership and what is not. This approach is not without biblical precedent. The apostle Paul did it on occasion, for example, when he wrote:

> Brothers, think of what you were when you were called. Not many of you were wise by human standards; not many were influential; not many were of noble birth. But God chose the foolish things of the world to shame the

wise; God chose the weak things of the world to shame the strong. He chose the lowly things of this world and the despised things—and the things that are not—to nullify the things that are, so that no one may boast before him.

It is because of him that you are in Christ Jesus, who has become for us wisdom from God—that is, our right-eousness, holiness and redemption. Therefore, as it is writ-ten: "Let him who boasts boast in the Lord."

When I came to you, brothers, I did not come with eloquence or superior wisdom as I proclaimed to you the testimony about God. For I resolved to know nothing while I was with you except Jesus Christ and him cruci-fied. I came to you in weakness and fear, and with much trembling. My message and my preaching were not with wise and persuasive words, but with a demonstration of the Spirit's power, so that your faith might not rest on men's wisdom, but on God's power. We do, however, speak a message of wisdom among the mature, but not the wis-dom of this age or of the rulers of this age, who are coming to nothing. (1 Corinthians 1:26–2:6, NIV)

The majority of leaders begin with a genuine heart to serve God and others. However, our sinful nature makes us ripe prey for the devil's lures.

If you are greatly gifted, you may be able to do marvelous things that would cause the public to be swept up in your skills and in your abilities. In the process of your growing, you will find great temptation to make a name for yourself, to make a big splash, to gain attention, to get the glory, to strut around, to increase your fees, to demand your rights, and to expect kid-glove treatment.[3]

The temptation that each of us faces is to cross out the word *servant* and underline *leader*. Reality, though, does not demand an either / or choice but a continuum that acknowledges the journey we are all traveling. In other words, we are not either a power leader or a servant leader, but we are at times one or the other, or somewhere between the two. So many of our leadership motivations, practices, and outcomes originate from who we are before God and where we are in our walk with Him.

The following is a list of characteristics that contrasts power leadership with servant leadership. It's helpful to see the distinctions between these two styles.

Power Leaders . . .	Servant Leaders . . .
• Feed on the spotlight	• Share the spotlight with others
• Are the focal point of the ministry	• Make Jesus the focal point
• Don't develop other leaders	• Develop many people
• Have a high turnover as people leave the ministry	• Have a low turnover because people stay and are loyal
• Keep the focus on themselves and their agenda	• Make Christ the central focus and agenda
• Cannot share agendas	• Affirm and participate in kingdom agendas
• Feed on being in charge and having power	• Are committed to being a servant first and foremost
• Leave people feeling hurt and abused	• Are committed to reconciliation and relationships
• Refer to their title frequently	• May have a title but seldom refer to it
• Are masters of manipulation and/or abuse those who get in their way	• Respect people for their freedom to think, act, and respond
• Use power images, offices, and perks to reveal their place	• Abhor the thought of using power images
• Pull rank to get their way	• Never abuse people or get their way only because of their position
• Recruit many followers for their work	• Develop many followers for the Lord

YOU CAN'T DO IT ALONE

Anyone marked by God for a leadership role faces tough questions almost hourly. Like Jesus, we must know when to overturn the moneychangers' tables and when to pick up the clay bowl and the towel. This means leading according to the dictates of the Holy Spirit and not by the dictates of an institution, organization, or by popular demand. This may mean stepping aside from leadership or submitting to another believer in a conflict.

Of course, this reality may not be well received by either the professional clergy *or* the laity. Institutionalism and professionalism have been the status quo for so long that for many they have become equivalent to divine authority.

Few would argue that we can live the Christ-centered life on our own. The truth is that we are made righteous by the unilateral act of Christ's sacrifice, and we begin to live by the unlimited sufficiency of Christ's presence. As we become progressively aware of our own weaknesses, experiencing brokenness and dependence, we will increasingly operate less in our own power, sufficiency, and strength, and will appropriate Christ's power, sufficiency, and strength. To live the gospel is to say, "I cannot do it myself. I have no power resident within me."

If this is to be the manner of the new life as a redeemed individual, then should not the same truths apply to the body of Christ at large? Isn't growth a matter of perceiving the limitations and weaknesses of our own ideas, strategies, and human wisdom, forsaking them in brokenness and acknowledging our increasing need of Him? Should we not vigorously examine our community's exercise of power and strength to see from where it is flowing: the flesh or the Father? Should we not cry out that we are helpless and have no means to accomplish the work of the kingdom apart from His empowerment?

"The way of the Christian leader is not the way of upward mobility in which our world has invested so much, but the way of downward mobility ending on the cross."[4] On that splintered wood almost two thousand years ago, a Servant Leader made Himself utterly helpless, completely weak and totally dependent. As a result, the gates of hell were rendered impotent and the gates of heaven opened, pouring its lasting power on a waiting world.

"As the Father has sent Me, I also send you," Jesus said toward the end of His earthly ministry (John 20:21). The Father sent Him to show the world what He was like, just, holy, forgiving, joyful, peaceful, kind, gentle, and patient. In the same manner, God sends us out into the world as leaders in His body, representing Him by shepherding, equipping, and serving.

Fortunately, He hasn't left us on our own to face such a challenge. We don't have to resort to the strategies of the world around us. We don't have to be the person in charge, motivating others through guilt and manipulation, letting tangible success be our guiding light. Jesus said, "These must not be so among you." There truly must be a different process in the body of Christ. And as leaders—spiritual leaders—God charges us with the responsibility to make sure it is a different process.

God promises us His power to meet the challenge. His power descended, embracing weakness and humility as the upward path. His power laid aside the vestiges of strength and position, choosing instead a basin filled with water to wash another's feet. What can we make of this One we follow, who calls us to lead as He led? It is not the path our instincts clamor for. But it's the only one that brings about true transformation in ourselves and in those we serve.

The body needs leaders who will move away from the temptations of ego, power, and control. We need leaders who will serve people and place their needs ahead of organizational structures or program goals; recognize their own gifting and the gifting of others in the body; and desire with deep passion to turn hearts to the One who has made them His.

If the body is to do more than limp along into the third millennium, she must have leaders who will return to their true calling—that of being the shepherds, servants, and equippers of the people of God.

Shepherd the flock of God which is among you, serving as overseers, not by compulsion but willingly, not for dishonest gain but eagerly; nor as being lords over those entrusted to you, but being examples to the flock; and when the Chief Shepherd appears, you will receive the crown of glory that does not fade away. (1 Peter 5:2-4, NKJV)

REFLECT ON YOUR LEADERSHIP

- Review the chapters of this book, particularly the "Respond to the Challenge" sections. Record a thought or two about how each chapter has affected your thinking.
- Now ask yourself, *What does God want me to do with this?*
- Share your thoughts with several other leaders you know.

Respond to the Challenge

Attempt to serve courageously as a powerful initiator of God's agenda, using His means alone.

■ ■ ■

By faith, Lord, I boldly submit to daily yielding as a powerful servant in order to bring all honor to You and none to myself in any way.

APPENDIX
Resources for Further Investigation

IF YOU ARE INTERESTED IN FINDING OUT MORE ABOUT SERVANT LEADER-ship—and exploring practical ways to implement it in your ministry—check out these additional resources.

Books

Breakthru Spiritual Gifts by Ralph Ennis
Breakthru Primary Roles by Ralph Ennis
These tools are best used in tandem to help confirm or direct a person in understanding his or her "best fit" in the body of Christ. We have used these tools extensively in CoMission and The Navigators. I commend them to you without reservation.

Acquire these books through Lead Consulting, PO Box 32026 Raleigh, NC 27622, (919)783-0354.

Church Without Walls by Jim Petersen
(NavPress, 1992)
With a worldwide perspective, Jim Petersen speaks as one who has "been there" among God's people in missions, slugging it out in the trenches among the lost. He says the primary purpose of the

church is to be among the lost. What hinders the spread of the gospel is often our own perspectives and traditions in the church. If the gospel is to spread in a culture, even our own, it will have to be done by the common person, the layperson. This army of witnesses will become the church without walls.

Committed Communities by Charles J. Mellis
(William Cary Library, 1976)
How could the lay movement proceed? An army of laymen and laywomen, released and effective in ministry to and among the lost, will only happen as these faith-walkers work in committed communities or bands. Mellis gives timeless insights into the biblical and historical rationale for such a movement.

The Community of the King by Howard A. Snyder
(InterVarsity, 1977)
This book offers a theology of the church in which the people of God can be in community and vibrantly released for ministry at the same time. Snyder urges us back to a biblical ecclesiology in which relationships are key.

The Equipping Pastor by R. Paul Stevens and Phil Collins
(The Alban Institute, 1993)
The church is stuck due to lack of emphasis on equipping God's people for service. This book includes many helpful graphs and thought-provoking ideas. It also has helpful sections on Trinitarian and servant leadership. The last chapter, "Liberating the Laity for Mission," is worth the price of the book.

Leadership in Christian Ministry by James E. Means
(Baker, 1989)
"Anyone who influences the lives of other church members or the decision-making process may be thought of as a leader, whether or not there is popular recognition of the fact," says Means. "Leadership that is compatible with scriptural guidelines can only be other-centered; it can never be leader-centered." Means presents many helpful insights regarding genuine biblical Christian leadership.

Paul's Idea of Community by Robert Banks
  (Eerdmans, 1988)
According to Banks, the big idea in Paul's view of community is
freedom. This freedom comes from the interdependence of the
members of the community and the practice of individual spiritual gifts. Included are many helpful word studies and thought-
provoking insights into the early church.

Recommended Church Consultants
Dr. Paul Ford
11805 Marquette NE
Albuquerque, NM 87123
(505)296-8568
Paul serves as an excellent speaker and church consultant. He can
help a church or ministry understand the Train-'n'-Release ministry of empowering the laity for effective ministry. He offers a
variety of seminars, such as: "The Leadership Re-Pioneering
Process," "Empowering Leadership," and "Seven Steps to Mobi-
lizing Spiritual Gifts."

Bill Thrall
Leadership Catalyst, Inc.
5060 N. 19th Ave. Suite 306
Phoenix, AZ 85015
(602)249-7000
Do you want to ignite character growth in the developing leaders
in your church or ministry? Bill Thrall and the staff of Leadership
Catalyst can complement your existing training with character-
development training.

NOTES

Chapter Two: Not So Among You

1. Henri J. M. Nouwen, *In the Name of Jesus: Reflections on Christian Leadership* (New York: Crossroads, 1989), p. 45.
2. Vance Packard, quoted in James M. Kouzes and Barry Z. Posner, *The Leadership Challenge* (San Francisco: Jossey-Bass, 1987), p. 26.
3. Ted W. Engstrom, *The Making of a Christian Leader* (Grand Rapids: Zondervan, 1976), p. 24.
4. David L. McKenna, *Power to Follow, Grace to Lead: Strategy for the Future of Christian Leadership* (Dallas: Word, 1989), pp. 14-15.
5. Myron Rush, *Management: A Biblical Approach* (Wheaton, Ill.: Victor, 1988), p. 11.
6. Paul A. Cedar, *Strength in Servant Leadership* (Waco, Tex.: Word, 1987), pp. 37-38.
7. Peter Block, *The Empowered Manager: Positive Political Skills at Work* (San Francisco: Jossey-Bass, 1987), pp. 30, 31.
8. Alister McGrath, "A Better Way: The Priesthood of All Believers" in *Power Religion: The Selling Out of the Evangelical Church?* ed. Michael Scott Horton (Chicago: Moody, 1992), p. 309.
9. Philip Greenslade, *Leadership, Greatness and Servanthood* (Minneapolis: Bethany, 1984), p. 3.

Chapter Three: The Dark Side of Leadership

1. Henri J. M. Nouwen, *In the Name of Jesus: Reflections on Christian Leadership* (New York: Crossroads, 1989), p. 58.
2. Michael Scott Horton, "What This Book Is and Is Not" in *Power Religion: The Selling Out of the Evangelical Church?* (Chicago: Moody, 1992), p. 14.
3. James E. Means, *Leadership in Christian Ministry* (Grand Rapids: Baker, 1989), p. 41.
4. Howard A. Snyder, *Signs of the Spirit: How God Reshapes the Church* (Grand Rapids: Academie Books, 1989), p. 312.
5. Nouwen, p. 60.
6. Snyder, *Liberating the Church: The Ecology of Church and Kingdom* (Downers Grove, Ill.: InterVarsity, 1983), p. 252.
7. David Johansen and Jeff VanVonderen, *The Subtle Power of Spiritual Abuse: Recognizing and Escaping Spiritual Manipulation and False Spiritual Authority Within the Church* (Minneapolis: Bethany, 1991), pp. 112-113.
8. Means, p. 119.

Chapter Five: Understand This Cycle!

1. See John 2:14-16; Matthew 23; Mark 12:38-40; Luke 20:45-47.
2. Kenneth Scott Latourette, *A History of Christianity, Volume 1: Beginnings to 1500* (San Francisco: Harper, 1975), pp. 112-113.

3. Jim Petersen, *Church Without Walls: Moving Beyond Traditional Boundaries* (Colorado Springs: NavPress, 1992), p. 95.
4. Bruce Shelley, *Church History in Plain Language* (Waco, Tex.: Word, 1982), p. 85.
5. Latourette, p. 117.
6. Latourette, pp. 129-131.
7. Petersen, p. 93.
8. Snyder, p. 271.

Chapter Six: Theological Foundations
1. J. I. Packer, "Trinitarianism" in the New Bible Dictionary quoted in *The Equipping Pastor* (Washington, D. C.: The Alban Institute, 1993), p. 104.
2. Shared at the "North American Christian Leaders Prayer Summit" held in Portland, Oregon, on August 19-21, 1993.

Chapter Seven: Superstars or Saints?
1. Lawrence O. Richards and Clyde Hoeldke, *A Theology of Church Leadership* (Grand Rapids: Zondervan, 1980), p. 49.
2. David L. McKenna, *Power to Follow, Grace to Lead: Strategy for the Future of Christian Leadership* (Dallas: Word, 1989), p. 25.
3. James E. Means, *Leadership in Christian Ministry* (Grand Rapids: Baker, 1989), p. 109.
4. Means, p. 32.
5. Richard J. Foster, *Celebration of Discipline* (San Francisco: Harper and Row, 1978), pp. 110-118.

Chapter Eight: Awakening the Sleeping Giant
1. Colin Kruse, *New Testament Models of Ministry* (Nashville: Thomas Nelson, 1983), p. 186.
2. Philip Greenslade, *Leadership, Greatness and Servanthood* (Minneapolis: Bethany, 1984), p. 85.
3. Jim Petersen, *Church Without Walls: Moving Beyond Traditional Boundaries* (Colorado Springs: NavPress, 1992), p. 60.

Chapter Nine: Let My People Go!
1. F. F. Bruce in his classic book, *The Training of the Twelve,* amply proves this point.
2. Charles W. Colson and Ellen Santilli Vaughn, *The Body* (Dallas: Word, 1992), p. 282.

Chapter Ten: How Will You Unleash Them?
1. Robert Banks, *Paul's Idea of Community: The Early House Churches in Their Historical Setting* (Grand Rapids: Eerdmans, 1988), p. 131.
2. Banks, pp. 107-108.

Chapter Eleven: Faith and Courage
1. Max Lucado, *And the Angels Were Silent* (Portland, Ore.: Multnomah, 1992), p. 11.
2. Philip Greenslade, *Leadership, Greatness and Servanthood* (Minneapolis: Bethany, 1984), p. 142.
3. Charles Swindoll, *Living Above the Level of Mediocrity: A Commitment to Excellence* (Waco, Tex.: Word, 1987), p. 40.
4. Henri J. M. Nouwen, *In the Name of Jesus: Reflections on Christian Leadership* (New York: Crossroads, 1989), p. 63.

ABOUT THE AUTHOR

STACY RINEHART currently oversees The Navigators ministries in the U.S. cities. He has fulfilled numerous responsibilities with The Navigators since 1976. Most recently he led a partnership of thirty top trainers from ten denominations and ministry organizations who were given the task of developing and implementing the training and materials for the CoMission in the former Soviet Union.

The CoMission experience incorporated the full expression of this book. CoMission is a partnership of ministries including Campus Crusade, The Navigators, Walk Thru the Bible, Wesleyan World Mission, Association of Christian Schools International, OMS International, SEND International, Church of God—Anderson, Moody Bible Institute, Gospel Missionary Union, Christian and Missionary Alliance, Mission to the World, and many more— over eighty-four denominations and ministry organizations. Together, this group mobilized and sent over fifteen hundred laymen and laywomen from all walks of life to minister for one year each in the former Soviet Union.

Stacy's education includes a Master of Theology degree from Dallas Theological Seminary and a Doctor of Ministry degree from Trinity Evangelical Divinity School. He and his wife, Paula, have two children, Allison, 20, and Brady, 18. They reside in Raleigh, North Carolina.

Stacy has co-authored two previous books with Paula— *Choices: Finding God's Way in Sex, Singleness, and Marriage* (NavPress, revised 1996) and *Living for What Really Matters* (NavPress, 1986).

GREAT LEADERSHIP RESOURCES.

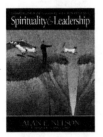